Tony Sibson
wishes this book to be dedicated
to his father and mother,
Keith and Kathleen.

Also by Jim Kirkwood, 2011
The Dartford Destroyer
The Life and Career of Dave Charnley
British, Empire and European Champion
Foreword by Norman Giller

Sibbo

The Tony Sibson Story
*Former British, European and
Commonwealth Champion*

Jim Kirkwood

Foreword by Bob Mee

Dalcumly Press

First published in the UK in 2013

Dalcumly Press
10 Forest Grove
Kilmarnock, Ayrshire KA3 1UP

ISBN 978-0-9569253-1-2

Typeset in Adobe Garamond, designed and produced by
Gilmour Print, www.self-publish-books.co.uk

Contents

Foreword

It is a privilege to write the foreword for this long overdue biography of Tony Sibson. I had a crack at it nearly twenty five years ago and I'm delighted that the legal complications that led to the scrapping of that venture have dissolved as time has gone by and look forward to reading the book and rekindling the memories of watching Tony fight all those years ago.

Maybe it was because we were born and raised in the same city at roughly the same time that gave us some initial common ground but after getting to know him as a fighter I found Tony Sibson the man a pleasure to be around. He's honest, open and generous of spirit – and I think that's why so many people loved to watch him fight. Whether he won or lost – and mostly, of course, he won – he gave of himself.

As with anyone, sometimes there was only so much he could give and he fell short but his fans knew he would always do everything within his considerable limits to provide value for money. He was as loyal to them, even on the occasions when some of them didn't deserve it, as they were to him.

It's easy to forget just how young he was in those far off days in the second half of the 1970s. He turned professional on his eighteenth birthday at Digbeth Civic Hall in Birmingham. I wasn't there that night but saw plenty of him as his fans followed him in increasing numbers to Wolverhampton, Wakefield, back at home in the De Montford Hall in Leicester, and on to the great nights at Wembley and the Royal Albert Hall. He had the speed of youth, bravery to spare and a left hook to dream of.

I'll never forget the night after his 21st birthday when he won the British middleweight title. Frank Lucas was a red-hot favourite, a snarling unhinged figure who brought marauding excitement and a heavy punch as well as the ability to break a man up with body shots. Sibson, however, understood this kind of crazy-man stuff. He refused to be intimidated and from the first bell took the fight to him with surging attacks. I was ringside for Boxing News, with my nose virtually on the ring apron, and remember Lucas with a kind of fury only just under control, smashing away at Sibson's body. I remember exchanging glances with Harry Mullan and both of us said later the other was wincing as those shots went in – and then suddenly Sibson showed just how good he was, a superb short left hook rocking Lucas as he poured it on. Sibson flicked the switch, went into overdrive, floored Lucas three times and won the title.

Of course, that was just the beginning of the story. I remember him weight drained against Kevin Finnegan, a boxer he idolised, but still just falling short over fifteen long rounds.

There was the sensational three round defeat of Alan Minter, which the public missed because of an advertising row, and then the heady nights in the USA. The naivety that surrounded his shot at Marvin Hagler for the world title on that incredibly snowy night in Worcester, Massachusetts, and his engaging, no-excuses reaction to it. The wrecking job on John Collins in Atlantic City when his whole career was on the line. The points win over Louis Acaries in the Bercy Stadium, Paris and the sad nights later on against Dennis Andries, and last of all, Frank Tate.

I had no doubts at all that the young Sibson would have destroyed Tate, as talented as the former Olympian from Texas was, but by then his love of boxing had been drained away by too many punches, too much experience of the way the business works at the top end, and well, by the fact that the craziness and eagerness to please that comes with youth had been replaced by the responsibilities of providing for a family of his own and by the natural process of growing up and appreciating what happens when you get hit on the head. By the time he fought Tate boxing had all but been knocked out of him.

We often talked about music; he said he liked Jimi Hendrix, the extravagant, loud showman, the excitement of the great man's guitar playing, yes, but perhaps more tellingly, the slow, sensitive parts of albums like Electric Ladyland and Axis Bold As Love.

Years later I listened as Mike Tyson gave one of his compelling monologues in a quiet moment before he fought Lennox Lewis. He put into words better than anyone I've ever known the reality of what it feels like to be alone in the ring when you really don't want to be there. I think Tony Sibson, or at least the one who fought Tate, would have identified with Tyson's words "Fighters have things to cry about. The pressure of fighting. It drives you crazy. Some guys do crazy things. It's all very well calling a fighter a nut but you don't know the pressure he has of getting bashed upside the head in front of all those people."

Sibson should be remembered alongside Alan Minter, Kevin Finnegan and Bunny Sterling as one of the golden quartet who dominated the British middleweight title in the 1970s, and Sibson, younger than the other three, went on to be the biggest drawcard of the next generation as well. He beat Mark Kaylor and had no doubts he would have repeated an old amateur success over Herol Graham if they had fought as professionals. "I'd have played piano on his ribs" he said at the time.

We can all look back on our youth with unrealistic fondness, elevating people above their worth, but the late 70s and early 80s were great years to be around boxing, they really were. There were so many very good fighters and it was, of course, a time when to be the best, boxers really did have to fight the best. In today's world where expectations of a boxer are so very different I have no doubt that Sibson would have held one of the world titles that are available. Knowing his tendency to dip in and out of form, it's likely that he would have won, lost, and regained one and kept us all on the edge of our seats, just as he used to do back in the 70s and 80s.

I know for Jim Kirkwood this process has been a labour of love. From the time he has spent first in persuading Tony to overcome his modesty and reticence and go back once more through those half-remembered, twenty-something days, and then once again in writing this book. To do it, he's had to be tenacious, patient and single-minded but I'm pleased he has succeeded in transferring the story to the page. I admire his dedication.

Jim's timely, very welcome biography of Dave Charnley obviously gave him a taste for writing and the addition of Tony's story to the books on boxing history is, I've no doubt, a super follow-up.

I know there are plenty of people out there who saw the Sibson career evolve who will want to relive those years and at the same time learn more about the man behind the fighter they saw and applauded. Hopefully, too, there will be a new generation of readers who have heard the name, *Tony Sibson*, mentioned in conversations, or read his record, and who will be pleased to have the opportunity to read the whole story of his career in one fascinating book.

I know, too, how difficult this whole process will have been for Tony Sibson himself. Outside of a boxing ring he's not the sort of man to seek out the spotlight and to have had to re-examine the highs and lows will have at one moment been excruciatingly embarrassing and at another emotionally painful.

Well, I for one am glad you decided to run with it, Tony.

Finally may I wish everyone involved with the production of this book the greatest success.

Bob Mee, *Snitterfield, Warwickshire, November 2012.*

Acknowledgments

Without the assistance of Tony and Bob Mee it would have been extremely difficult to get this book to the printers. In the late 80s, just as Tony's career came to an end, Bob put together an excellent book, but due to circumstances at the time it never went beyond the manuscript stage and was left to gather dust in Tony's sister Karen's house. When I started out on this project I didn't know of its existence, it was only when I contacted Bob with my ideas that it was revealed. Not surprisingly, given the character of the man, Bob immediately gave me permission to use all or any part of his previous work. I have used many quotes from that manuscript and it acted as an invaluable reference throughout my preparations. I am very grateful to Bob, and of course, there was nobody else more appropriate to write the foreword. Thanks again, Bob

The quiet man that Tony is, and his natural reticence to engage with complete strangers, caused me concerns when I started out with my research. I needn't have bothered. I had hours upon hours of face-to-face interviews and telephone conversations with Tony, the content of which have taken me, and hopefully you, behind the scenes and into the mind of the boxer himself. I know that since I started Tony has had many sleepless nights as he struggled with the twin aim of not upsetting anyone, but also ensuring complete accuracy with his recollections. Of course, we all have to realise that you can't fight at the very top level as a professional, with the huge amounts of money involved, without disagreements, misunderstandings and the realisation of how impersonal the boxing business can be, and all of this must leave scars. But, both Tony and I have tried to be as balanced as we possibly can.

To be frank, the most enjoyable aspect of writing a biography, is the *getting to know* the subject on a personal level, and I've often asked myself, even though this is only my second attempt, what would happen if I suddenly realised I didn't like the guy? Well, with both Tony and Dave Charnley, that was never an issue, you couldn't meet nicer people. Thanks for your help, Tony.

Another pleasure I had was meeting Ken Squires. There might be a realisation as you go through the book that I have a soft spot for Ken and that would be no accident. I'm convinced that without Ken, Tony's career would not have lasted as long as it did, nor would we have seen Tony at his best. More importantly for the book however, was Ken's willingness to help, his memory for detail and his forthright honesty. Mind you, this same *working class* need to call it, as he sees it, meant that some of what he said had to be omitted, to save the not so innocent! I hope we stay friends long after this is all over.

We should not forget that Carl Gunns was Tony's manager for an amazing 60% of his fights and that he was the man who set the ball rolling. It was as a result of Tony's actions inside the ring, and Gunns' outside it, which brought the British middleweight title home to Leicester. There was some acrimony when their professional relationship came to an end, but up until then both needed each other. Carl was unwell when I met him and we weren't able to go into as much detail as we might have wished, but I'm grateful for his assistance and I know he's feeling a lot better now.

Tony's lifelong buddy Mickey Bell, and his siblings, Craig, Troy and Sean, as well as sons Ryan, Nathan and daughter Jody all made their contributions. But I need to signal out sister Karen whose help with telephone numbers, family photographs and the family perspective in having a famous relative, were all important and helpful. Tony also wants me to acknowledge his other son, Carl, who he didn't become aware of until later years and whose mother's pride ensured that her son was brought up without her taking the perhaps easy route of seeking assistance from his famous father.

Pat Grundy, a lady who I've actually never met, did a great job for me by researching every issue of the Leicester Mercury newspaper between 1976 and 1988, and re-producing articles which have assisted me in getting a more local perspective as Tony's career progressed. I'm also very grateful for the assistance given to me by Richard Whiting at Action Images who allowed me to use photographs from their portfolio, especially the one on the front cover which I think looks very apt.

No one can write a boxing biography without the help of the trade paper, the Boxing News. From 1909 until the present day the paper comes out each week and prides itself on being an accurate record of boxing in this country and beyond. Down through the years their staff have maintained the highest standards of journalistic integrity, which means, for me at any rate, that what's written in the paper can be trusted to be factual, and further research can largely be ignored.

Once again, Douglas Gilmour at Gilmour Print has taken

my writings, photographs, jumbled up ideas and put together this book which I know at least *looks*, professional! I hope the content matches his high standards.

Finally, when I get an idea into my head it seems to dominate most of my days. The one who suffers most is *the wife*, Edna. I don't know how many times during my work for the book that she has told me something important, which at a later date I've denied ever having any knowledge. That's because I was generally walking about in a daze trying to word the next paragraph just so it reads right! We've been married thirty-five years and she's had to suffer a lot due to my unintentional deafness, but there you go. Thanks for your patience, life can get back to normal now. (When did you say we're going to Tesco?)

If I've missed anyone, I'm truly sorry, it wasn't intentional.

Hope you all enjoy the book.

Jim Kirkwood
Kilmarnock, 2013

Introduction

It's not as easy as some would think to give a book its title. After the long hours of research, the interpretation of interviews and dozens of phone calls, readers would be forgiven for thinking that selecting what's written on the front cover should be a relatively simple and straight forward process. After all, the biographer should by that time, have a clear understanding of who they've written about. But, it's not that simple.

From virtually the start of Tony Sibson's career, his Midlands based fans came up with the *Sibbo* nickname, and this stuck with him until the end. It was adopted by newspaper and magazine writers, boxing promoters and television commentators. It was attached to him like *bread* is to *butter*. Giving this title to his biography would instantly appeal to fans from that era, and be recognisable to countless others, particularly his own townsfolk in Leicester.

There is a different train of thought however. This follows the idea, that in some clever way, the title, in a few short words, should give potential readers a glimpse into the character of the book's subject. If I was to choose this route then the apparently simple task becomes much more difficult. One possible title might have read *The Enigma of the Ring*, which would have been fairly accurate, but this was used by Nat Fleischer when he wrote about Gene Tunney in 1931. My own preference would have been to call the book *Reluctant Hero*, but that, for me, sounds more like a title for a work of fiction – perhaps there even is such a book?

Sibbo was certainly an enigma in the ring, and a reluctant hero out with it, and I hope this comes across, as readers progress through the book. Notwithstanding the emotions of the man, the book will attempt to bring to life his boxing exploits more than anything else, and illustrate the sense of excitement generated whenever the *big punching* middleweight entered a boxing ring. There have been many boxers who have worn the European, Commonwealth and British crowns, and fought for world titles, and they are welcome to our sincere congratulations. Sibson, however, along with a handful of others, had that extra something – he could punch like a *wrecking ball* on a demolition site!

Boxing used to be called the *noble art*, a term meant to persuade the public to accept that there was a high level of skill used by eighteenth century practitioners, elevating them above ruffians brawling in the streets! Amongst boxing purists today there can still, quite rightly, be an emphasis on teaching defensive abilities, and there's no doubt there is much to be admired when watching a boxer who has mastered the art. But there is no getting away from the fact that nothing, I repeat, nothing, excites the boxing public more, and attracts the casual observer to show an interest, than a boxer who can knock people out. It's not nice, it can be dangerous, and it seems brutal to so many, but that doesn't make it any less truthful.

It's perhaps worthwhile to also suggest that Sibson was not part of the *one punch knockout* brigade. That extremely rare breed, seem to be born with such a talent, and are as rare as *hen's teeth*. No, Tony's blows were akin to those of the axe man – keep swinging until the tree falls! Sometimes the *tree* in question needs only a couple of strikes. On other occasions several more are required, but inevitably once the *axe*, starts to sink home, there is no doubt the tree is coming down! The analogy to *tree* and *axes* will become relevant as the reader goes through the book.

In the latter half of his career, Sibson's bludgeoning style became a good deal more sophisticated. The hard punching remained, and so too did his tendency to continue marching forward, but observations show that his ability to avoid blows was an understated aspect of his performances. This fact is borne out today in the absence of any long lasting facial damage, bar thin, linear scars on his eyelids. He was able to move his head a fraction of an inch, just enough to avoid incoming punches, and if that wasn't good enough, then his hand or shoulder was in position to deflect them out of harm's way. To do this regularly while moving into range, and usually against much taller opponents, is testament to the effort Tony and his trainers put in to the technical aspects of his game.

There is a lot more to Sibson's character than what was exposed in a boxing ring. Occasionally the emotional issues would rise to the surface, to be seen and heard, possibly in the immediate aftermath of a traumatic ring battle. On other occasions they might have been alluded to in print, interpreted by journalists who were fortunate enough to get close to *the reluctant hero*. This book will explore the complex relationships he had with managers, trainers and promoters and give us an insight into how these worked both for and against a young man who became traumatised by a business he never fully understood and accepted.

Many people at the time, thought, wrongly, that Tony and his family were *travellers* and while preparing for the book, I met many others who still think that today. The Sibson family knew this, and had many a laugh about it, blaming Tony's dad, Keith, who was the cause of the speculation due to his lifestyle. While Tony might not have had a *Romany* background he does have many of the traits expected of those with that lifestyle. He seems unable to live in the one place for too long, and has difficulty living a routine life with deadlines and appointments. He likes to be spontaneous, and is reluctant to plan too far ahead. It's just the way he is! Boxing was the foundation for a successful life in business, and he's thankful for the life boxing gave him. He is extremely grateful to those loyal supporters who followed him everywhere, even across the Atlantic Ocean and English Channel. But he doesn't miss the, *old fight game.*

I don't know why, but many of us seem to think that our sporting heroes from yesteryear, hanker back for the *good old days*, when they were celebrities, and media people were constantly hounding them for interviews. We also like to think that they are still involved in their sport to some degree, perhaps just to the extent of reading about it or watching on the television. It came as a shock to me when interviewing Dave Charnley in my previous effort at writing a biography, that Dave had little interest in boxing, and to be frank, it was only when the book was complete and the book signings started, that his old passion for the sport re-emerged. I had a similar experience when I first met Tony. There was a reluctance to bring his previous boxing memories back to life, and although Tony had not distanced himself from boxing as much as Dave, he nevertheless shared a belief that what he did was nothing special.

Well, I have to disagree, and I hope you do too!

CHAPTER 1

From Small Beginnings

When looking back to 1958 with our modern understanding of acceptable standards of living it's an inescapable fact that when Tony Sibson was born on 9 April that year he entered a world which would be unrecognisable today. He was the first born to Keith and Kathleen who at that time lived in Bardolph Street, to the north east of Leicester city centre. There's was a mid terraced house in a deprived section of the city with no hot water and a shared outside toilet next to the coal sheds.

But, like many from that era and background, Sibson is not ashamed or embarrassed in any way. In fact he's proud of his heritage and would not have had it any other way. It was a rough, tough neighbourhood which has long since been demolished. Over the succeeding seven years Keith and Kathleen presented Tony with three younger brothers and a sister. Brand new clothes for the family were a luxury the young Sibson's didn't experience relying on *hand-me-downs* from wealthier relatives and from what Tony refers to as the *rag and bone bag*.

Dad, Keith, didn't have a normal *everyday* type job, but he always worked and provided for his growing family. Tony describes him as a *dealer*. He was often away from home with travelling horse fairs and bought and sold anything he could get his hands on. On one occasion the young Tony remembers coming home to find a horse in the back yard! On another occasion Keith had a pig sty on a nearby waste area known as the *Black Pad*.

Tony had very little interest in school and there were clear reasons for this. On the one hand there were neither relatives, friends nor neighbours who progressed to higher education and could have acted as role models to encourage formal learning. Perhaps more significantly was the young Sibson's personality. He was painfully shy and would not have enjoyed the attention of teachers during lessons. He would have had difficulty speaking up in class. Added to this, was a restlessness and a strong desire to be outside with his pals, all of which acted as a deterrent to even a comprehensive level of schooling. By the time he arrived at Rushey Meads High School the pattern was set and over a period of time his teachers realised he was having difficulty with reading. Tony's sister Karen describes him as being a slow reader and a very poor writer at that time. In fact when he first became well known, he used to practice writing his autograph because he was a bit envious when he saw other boxers signing their names with a flourish!

Tony had always tried to do odd jobs to earn extra cash, but his first real step into employment was as a hod carrier to his bricklaying uncle Peter when he was fourteen. To anyone not familiar with what hod carrying involved within the building trade in those days an explanation might be worthwhile. A hod was a *V* shaped piece of wood with a shaft fixed underneath to hold it steady. On the *V* would be placed a number of bricks or concrete *breeze blocks* and the hod carrier would be required to transport these on his shoulder to wherever the bricklayer was working, sometimes climbing ladders up several floors. It was

not a job for weaklings and it is no surprise that the left handed
Sibson developed a devastating punch with this arm.

Of course this money making enterprise was a further
distraction from school and his attention to lessons continued
in a downward spiral to point that when he reached sixteen he
departed the school playground like a shot out of a gun!
Surprisingly his first job was not in the building trade but at W
and J Parkers Ltd an abattoir near the cattle market in Leicester.

By this time Sibson was an established amateur boxer and
had fought for the Young England team. His family had a
background in boxing with his grandfather Wally Sibson being
a professional lightweight. He fought under the pseudonym
Colin McDonald and had twenty one fights between November
1925 and February 1934. Bizarrely he also wore the *Star of
David* on his shorts claiming it would get him more fights! Even
more surprising for a Leicester man, having his first professional
fight, his debut was at the famous National Sporting Club in
Covent Garden, London. Wally was well known locally as a man
who engaged in hundreds of fights in the old boxing booths
which were popular at travelling fairgrounds. A larger than life
character who wore his jet black hair longer than normal for the
period stayed in boxing as a top class referee.

It's not unusual therefore to understand why the young
eleven years old Sibson joined the Thurmaston Amateur Boxing
Club, situated upstairs in the Working Mens Club of the same
name. However it was when he moved to the nearby Belgrave
Amateur Boxing Club, also situated above a working men's club,
that he came under the watchful eye of Jim Knight. It was then
that the young Sibson began to emerge as a top fighter in the

making. Tony's great pal from those days, Mickey Bell, had a high regard for the trainer and recalled what the gym was like. "Jim Knight was a hard man, a bull terrier. He taught Tony how to throw the left hook. You could see the improvement. Carl Gunns was there as the matchmaker and Jack and Ernie Fenton were also trainers at the club along with Ken Squires. Ernie's sons Steve and Eddie were there with Tony and me as well as my brother Billy. Tony wasn't a particular stand out but I'd say he was above average at that time. Remember he was in with a good bunch of fighters."

Mickey Bell himself would go on to have twenty one fights as a professional in a two year career during which he fought for the Scottish light-welterweight title due to his family originally hailing from Dumfries, and lost his last fight to Sylvester Mittee a future British and Commonwealth champion.

By his mid-teens, around the time he fought for the Young England team, Tony and some of his Belgrave club members were training like professionals. Mickey remembered those days well. "We were training on Sunday morning, Monday, Wednesday and Friday nights at the Belgrave and Jim Knight had us down at the gym above the Jolly Angler pub on Tuesday and Thursday nights with his pros. He had Tim Wood and the heavyweight Rocky Campbell there at the time. We were sparring these types of guys."

Jim Knight had a good squad of heavyweights at his Jolly Angler gym, although in the present day they would have been fighting in the cruiserweight division which at that time hadn't been introduced. Campbell would win the Midlands area heavyweight title; Tim Wood became British light heavyweight champion and Eddie Fenton won the Midlands title. Another Belgrave boxer, who later had a very successful professional career, was Tony McKenzie who had the highest regard for Jim Knight's skills. "He was the man! He was the Freddie Roach of his day."

Ken Squires, who later become Sibson's trainer, remembered those days at the Belgrave with great pride. "I was asked to come over to help train at the Belgrave from Syston. There was Jim Knight as well as Jack and Ernie Fenton who had been at the Thurmaston club. We had a great bunch of lads. The best of the lot was Dougie Ralston from over by Coalville. He was a bit older than Tony, but we knew Tony was a bit special. We showed him how to swing out to the left, shuffle his front foot forward and throw the left hook to either the head or the body. We had a lot of good boxers so the sparring helped them all."

All through the time Sibson was at the Belgrave the matchmaker was Carl Gunns. Gunns said that Sibson never complained about who he had to fight. It was simple, Gunns picked the opponent and Sibson fought him. A meticulous record keeper, Gunns reported that Sibson took part in 102 amateur fights with eighty-two as a senior. He had a better than average record winning fifty-seven of those fights.

Mickey Bell remembered an important milestone in Sibson's amateur career at a Midlands Area Southern Zone ABA qualifying event when Tony was seventeen. Tony fought another Midlander Harry Watson. "I'm telling you, Tony won that fight, it was close, but he won it. I think they gave it to Watson because he had been beaten in the final the year before. Later that night Watson fought Paul Shutt from our club and was knocked out, but Tony had taken all the fight out of him. I lost my fight to

Pat Cowdell." Bell felt that this poor decision caused a fair degree of resentment in Sibson and pushed him eventually towards turning professional.

Because of their connections through the gym, Mickey, Tony and the others used to socialise with each other. "We used to feed Tony's dad's pigs up at the *Black Pad*, and we'd listen for hours to Johnny Cash records. Johnny Cash was a hero to Tony and he eventually met him in America. He told me that Cash was a big man with huge hands. I could tell you a hundred stories about what we got up to in those days but you couldn't print them. We had a great laugh. I know that people think that Tony's shy, and he is with strangers, but he would have been the leader in our little gang."

This friendship turned up an amazing coincidence for both of them. Mickey kept chickens at his house and a local man showed him how to slaughter and clean them. This man recommended him for a job at Parkers abattoir and on his first morning at his new job he bumped into Tony who had independently also been given a start that day. Mickey still has this job almost forty years later, while the constant damp and cold conditions drove Sibson away much sooner.

Tony discussed this first step into formal working life with journalist Bob Mee. "We would kill hundreds of sheep on a Friday morning. It was one sort of animal one day, one on another, and so on. There were so many it used to drive me mad. You just didn't think. I look back and I can't believe I ever did it. I love animals, but it was a job and I needed it. I was young and I would do anything. When you're young, you just do it. You never look at anything you do. But it got to the point where I was getting nowhere. And in the slaughterhouse it was freezing. I can't tell you how cold it was. There were fridges everywhere. You were always wet because everything had to be washed down all the time. It was always too cold. At least in the building, I thought, you had a chance of keeping yourself warm. You were better off outside than freezing in there."

Just after Tony turned seventeen, around the summer of 1975, George Biddles a very famous and influential Midlands manager suggested to Carl Gunns that he should consider taking out a boxing manager's licence. Gunns was relatively young to take on this role. However Biddles had already identified Sibson as a potential star in the professional game, and had seen something in Gunns which made him think the two of them could work well together. Gunns broached the subject with the young Sibson and, with the help of Biddles, eventually obtained his licence from the Midlands Area Council.

Tony had become disillusioned by the amateur game. The loss to Watson had been the final straw. He realised as well that he was training like a professional without the benefits of earning money from his fights. He could overhear conversations about the money the older professionals at the Jolly Angler were getting on a regular basis and his friends at the Belgrave were beginning to consider taking this path. He had been sparring with seasoned professionals for years and he knew he could at least hold his own with them. At the same time Carl Gunns felt he had went as far as he could in his role as an amateur matchmaker and accepting the persuasive words of George Biddles can recall Tony signing on with him as his manager over an orange juice at a time when others were hovering around trying to snap up the exciting young amateur star.

Although Sibson had achieved a degree of success in fighting for Young England, he did not have a particularly outstanding record but had a style which the discerning eye could recognise as being more suited to professional boxing. The expertise of George Biddles was influential in this. He knew that as Sibson matured his punch power would increase simultaneously, and understood there is nothing the average boxing fan enjoys more, than to follow a knockout artist! Sibson had his last amateur contest on Saturday 21 February 1976, as a supporting bout at the Midland Counties ABA finals in Derby Sports Centre, where he stopped local lad D Powell in the second round.

Some thirty-five years later Sibson recalled his own feelings at the time." Listen, we turned professional more as laugh, a dare, than anything else. We all went at around the same time. We thought we'd earn some money, nothing else. I never wanted any of that nonsense that happened later. I just wanted to go to the fights with my mates and have a bit of fun."

It's without doubt that Sibson could not have envisaged how long his professional boxing career would last, nor how successful, and famous, he'd become. George Biddles would ultimately be proved correct and Carl Gunns grateful that he too accepted his advice. It should also not be forgotten the influence Sibson's father, Keith, had on his son's fledgling boxing career. Keith had a dominant position within his family and Tony's sister Karen can recall how it was their father who encouraged, persuaded and sometimes threatened the youngster to attend his training sessions when he appeared to need a night off. Keith's support for his son would be a permanent feature throughout the next twelve years.

CHAPTER 2

Learning His Trade

There were no fanfares or media conferences when Tony Sibson turned professional. Why should there have been? He was a good amateur but had never won an ABA title, never won an Olympic or Commonwealth medal and had lost his fair share of contests. He had boxed for Young England but Sibson explained how he viewed that outing. "Young England were due to fight Ireland, and the lad in the Irish team was a European champion or something. They didn't want the top English lad fighting him so I was called in."

Sibson had enough of winning prizes and losing debatable decisions and thought he might as well earn some cash from fighting. There was nothing more to it than that. There were no grand ambitions and no thoughts of winning titles. At the same time new manager Carl Gunns felt he'd had enough of amateur boxing. He'd organised forty-eight shows for the Belgrave club and made hundreds of matches for the boxers, travelling all over the country. He felt it was time for a new adventure.

On 31 March 1976 Sibson's former Belgrave teammate, Steve Fenton, managed coincidentally by George Biddles, beat Liverpool's Charlie Richardson in his second fight as a professional. Fenton won easily enough flooring his experienced opponent in the second round. This may have influenced Carl Gunns, not yet recognised by the Board of

Control as Sibson's manager, to have a re-think about who his young protégé should have as his first opponent. He had originally been due to face Gareth Jones.

Nine days later, on his eighteenth birthday, Tony did, in fact, make his debut against Richardson but only after his opponent had squeezed in another contest, and another defeat, four days previously. Nowadays boxers must have a minimum of seven days between fights but that was not the case then. The first fight was at Digbeth Civic Hall on the undercard of the Midlands heavyweight title fight between Eddie Fenton, Steve's brother, who also trained at the Jolly Angler, and Garfield McEwan.

Sibson as expected came out quick and had Richardson down with a right hand in the first round. The Scouser came out swinging wildly in the second and was quickly floored with a flurry of hooks before the mismatch was halted by referee John Coyle at the one minute forty-six seconds mark of a fight scheduled for six, two minute rounds. Richardson had only one more fight after this before calling it a day.

The Leicester group were buoyed by Tim Wood's narrow victory over Phil Martin on 28 April which won him the British light-heavyweight crown, and this brought national recognition to the Leicester boxing community.

Promoter Dave Roden put on his first show at Birmingham's National Exhibition Centre on 6 May attracting an attendance of about 2, 500. Both Tony and another ex Belgrave amateur, Dougie Ralston were on the show and both won well. Ralston stopped his opponent in the second round but Sibson had to go the full six rounds distance with Belfast's John Breen. Breen just made it to the final bell after a late Sibson onslaught, stumbling into the referee at the final bell. This had been a good match for Sibson as Breen was having his eighth fight, having won six of his first seven.

A noticeable gimmick with the young Sibson was his wearing of long, almost knee length, boxing trunks, ran up on a sewing machine by his Auntie Pearl. This was in the days when shorts worn by footballers and boxers were aptly named. One story had it that Tony's dad Keith, thinking of his own father's showmanship in wearing the Star of David on his trunks, introduced this idea to his son during his amateur days. Carl Gunns put forward a more practical suggestion. He says that Tony was built so powerfully from the waist up that he was embarrassed with his thin white legs and wanted them covered up! Perhaps the reality lies somewhere in between?

Sibson's next outing was on a Ron Gray promotion at Wolverhampton Civic Hall on 26 May against Liam White from Wells. This proved to be the Somerset man's third last fight and he came in with a record of twenty-two defeats from thirty-six contests. It's fair to say Sibson gave White a real thumping for six rounds, although a bit too reliant on his left hand. Sibson received a thunderous round of applause at the end.

By the middle of June Ron Gray had managed to put together a bill for the 14 July at Wolverhampton Civic Hall topped by Danny McAlinden against Eddie Fenton. Tony was pencilled in to fight Derek McCarthy with mates Steve Fenton and Dougie Ralston also scheduled to appear.

This turned out to be a bad night for the Belgrave men. Eddie Fenton was stopped in the fourth round after a blood bath, while his brother Steve lost for the first time on a cut eye to Leroy

Herriott. Sibson brought some cheer with a hard fought points win over Pudsey's Jimmy Pickard. It was Pickard's seventh fight, having three wins and three losses in his previous six. One of those defeats was to another ex –Belgrave fighter, Paul Shutt, in May. Sibson suffered his first knockdown near the end of the third and was unsteady on rising. Tony backpedalled for most of the next two rounds before flooring Pickard in the last to secure the win.

Following the summer break Sibson returned slightly overweight at 11st 10lb for his match at Digbeth Civic Hall on 10 September. His Welsh opponent Patrick *Bonny* McKenzie was also coming into the fight unbeaten. Sibson started smartly but McKenzie began to come into it from the third. The fight turned in the fifth round when the Cardiff fighter took a Sibson left hook leaving him scrambling on his knees and he never fully recovered. McKenzie went down again as the sixth ended and at one minute and ten seconds of the next round, with the stricken fighter wobbling about the ring, the referee wisely intervened. Tony remembered "Bonny McKenzie was a tough so-and-so. We fought three times. Every time he used to cling a bit – he was a spoiler more than anything, but he was very strong. A good fighter."

Sibson had a routine fight on 22 October again at Digbeth Civic Hall against Clive Davidson, a Londoner managed by Dennie Mancini. Davidson, really a light-middleweight, was outclassed being knocked down in both the seventh and eighth rounds and only just surviving to the bell. Tony wasn't too impressed with his performance and said afterwards "I just couldn't get it together tonight. I knew I had him but I just couldn't knock him out. I don't know why, maybe I am not experienced enough yet." The fight was put on last to ensure that, with the large following from Leicester, the Hall was still full at the end. That morning Carl Gunns' manager's licence arrived from the Board. It was remarkable that Gunns, who was after all still only thirty years of age, could find himself in this position. It was particularly young for this role, a factor which may have caused the delay in the Midlands Area Council granting his licence. But he was doing well in arranging suitable matches for his young protégé.

Looking back, Tony while reminiscing, had fond memories from this period. "They were great days. People used to come to my fights, get drunk, make friends and have a big party. All I was doing was jumping off the scaffold at dinner-time, having a kip in the afternoon and getting in there. I was coming out unscathed and I felt it was a way I could make people happy in return for the pleasure they gave me. I'm not very good in company, in a crowd I'll just stay on the edge, absorbing the atmosphere and enjoying it. But I blush if I have to say too much."

Twelve days later Paul Shutt and Tony travelled across country to Caister in Norfolk for fights at Neptune's Palace. Both returned from the seaside with victories. Sibson's opponent, Mancunian Neville Esteban, in his third fight, was no match for the Leicester boxer and was widely outpointed over eight rounds. Although reluctant to admit it, Sibson realised very quickly that his opponent was out of his depth and took things a bit gently. Strangely enough Esteban had his last fight two years later against future Sibson opponent, and world champion, Dennis Andries.

It was back to the Midlands on the last day of November at Dudley Town Hall for a rematch with Irishman John Breen. Breen was coming off a win outpointing the Northern Ireland light-heavyweight champion Tony Monaghan. Manager Gunns said at the time "Tony is very fit and I know he has the ability to beat Breen again. He is much taller than Tony but we are hoping to catch him with telling body punches." Sibson improved on his previous performance and stopped Breen in five rounds. The referee stepped in after Sibson had floored the visitor who was unable to defend himself. It was not all joy for the Leicester clan with Steve Fenton being stopped in the fourth round of his fight. As a sad footnote to this show it is worth remembering Tredegar middleweight Leroy Herriott who had been due to fight on the bill. Leroy had previously fought Steve Fenton and Dougie Ralston but two days before the promotion he was involved in a road accident, breaking his neck, leaving him paralysed.

With the end of the year approaching the Boxing News had Sibson ranked as their twelfth ranked middleweight in Britain, behind his next opponent Tim McHugh, a surprising position for the Birkenhead fighter given that he had lost his last seven fights. He had even lost his last fight to Tony's pal Paul Shutt. Their fight took place at the Gala Baths in West Bromwich on 14 December. Tony was roared on by a large following and took McHugh to the cleaners stopping the taller man in the fourth round. This win enthused Carl Gunns who told the local press that it had been Sibson's best performance yet, adding "He's still got a lot to learn, but he's surprised even me with the way he's progressed."

In a bizarre event, Leicester's Eddie Fenton's match with Brian Huckfield was abandoned when the overhead ring canopy caught fire due to close proximity of television lights.

With the last issue of 1976 the Boxing News included their annual top ten prospects article. Leading the pack was Kirkland Laing followed by Sibson and at number five they had Paul Shutt. Four lads from the Belgrave club had discarded their amateur vests this year, Sibson, Shutt, Steve Fenton and Dougie Ralston. Between them they'd taken part in twenty-six bouts, winning twenty-two. Fellow boxers from the Jolly Angler including Tim Wood and Eddie Fenton engaged in a further eleven fights with six victories, the most significant being Wood's annexation of the British title.

Nothing much had changed from his amateur days in terms of preparing for fights. Contrary to the Board's rule at that time, which banned professionals from training and sparring with amateurs, Tony was still working out at both the Belgrave club and the Jolly Angler under the watchful eye of Jim Knight. Preparation for contests was still pretty basic though. Carl Gunns certainly used his extensive knowledge of the boxing scene, not easy in the days before the internet, when he was arranging fights, but in terms of someone having overall control of Tony's training and tactics for his bouts, these were areas within which the lines of responsibility were blurred. Prior to his fights there were no real discussions on the particular attributes of his opponents and very little by way of tactical planning. Sibson reflected on the situation at the time. "People go on about this, nobody told me anything. We would see the kid at the weigh in and Jim would say 'see what's he's like, get in there have a look, straighten him out with some good jabbing', and that was it."

CHAPTER 3

Rising Star

It was becoming apparent in boxing circles that Sibson's star was on the rise. He was winning his fights in style and packing out small hall shows with his growing band of followers from Leicester and other areas of the Midlands. He was a godsend to the Midlands promoters, Ron Gray and Dave Roden, who could guarantee significant ticket sales when Tony was on the bill. Carl Gunns was getting in on the act by working hard in the Leicester area selling tickets and was benefitting from the commission these sales attracted.

With the dawn of the Queen's Silver Jubilee Year at the beginning of 1977, Carl Gunns had arranged a daunting schedule of four fights in six weeks. He told Ken Gaunt of the Leicester Mercury that Sibson thrived on hard work and if he didn't pick up any injuries he'd have four fights before the end of February, adding that there was a public demand for him because he gave value for money.

Sibson opened up the year on 11 January with a convincing win over Cardiff's Tony Burnett in a bout scheduled for eight rounds. Again, following a holiday break, Tony's weight was up at 11st 9lb for this show at Wolverhampton Civic Hall. Burnett was having his thirty-eighth fight, and with only thirteen wins over the previous seven years, hardly a stern challenge for the rising Leicester star. This was emphasized in the first minute when a left hook from Tony had him down, and there were calls from the crowd for the referee to stop it as the bout was reaching its conclusion.

In the middle of January the Midlands Area Council granted permission for Dave Roden to promote a show at De Montford Hall in Leicester on 24 March. Roden proposed a Leicester v The Rest bill featuring Sibson, Paul Shutt, Eddie Fenton, Derek Simpkin and Tony's great friend, Mickey Bell who had just turned professional. The Midlands decision had upset rival promoter Johnny Griffin who had also applied for that date and when Roden asked Griffin for the services of his fighter, Dougie Ralston, it was, perhaps understandably, declined.

On the Midlands Sporting Club show on 19 January at Solihull there was a double celebration with Tony and Mickey Bell, having his first contest, winning their fights. Sibson's opponent Roy Gumbs could punch, with three of his four wins to date coming inside the distance. Gumbs had a deceptively ordinary record as was proved later when he went on to win the British and Commonwealth middleweight titles, winning a Lonsdale Belt outright, five years later. In 1985 he would make an unsuccessful challenge for the International Boxing Federation world championship in the new super-middleweight division. Being Mickey Bell's first fight he remembered the day well. "Four of us went over in the car to Solihull, Jim Knight, Tony's dad Keith, me and him. It was an early weigh-in. After we'd weighed in Jim and Keith went away for a pint so we were left hanging about this town hall or something. We were starving and searched about until we found the kitchen. There was nothing there but we saw a fridge and looked inside. There was a box of ice cream blocks which were each wrapped round with paper to keep them together. Well there were twenty-four of these in this box and without a word of a lie, we ate the lot, all twenty-four, and we were fighting a few hours later. We had a right laugh about that."

Anyway, the temperamental Gumbs came out aggressively and in the first round had Tony under a bit of pressure, not surprising given that he had a dozen choc ices in his stomach! But from the second round onwards Sibson fought intelligently behind a stiff jab with follow-up hooks to control the action and ran out a convincing winner. Years later Sibson commented on the fight. "He could have been Joe Bloggs to me. None of the names mattered to me then. I just left Carl to do the matchmaking. He knew what he was doing –I don't remember worrying about who was in there with me. Gumbs caught me off guard in the first round with a right hand. He was an awkward fighter and he did shake me for the first time in my career. I was just used to doing what I wanted to do, but he made me think all the way through the fight. After about three rounds I got into my rhythm, though, and started to look into him and then just got on with my job."

Former heavyweight Johnny Prescott co-promoted at Tiffany's Ballroom in Coventry on 10 February and Sibson showed the power in his left hook when he stopped Draycott's Arthur Winfield in the second round. This was to be Winfield's second last fight and he'd already lost in November to former Belgrave amateur, Paul Shutt. At this time the boxing press seemed to be of a view that out of the Leicester lads, Shutt seemed to be the best prospect. He was ranked in the top ten in

Britain at light-middleweight and like Sibson was unbeaten. Manager Gunns enjoyed this event in particular because the promoter, Prescott, a former top level heavyweight boxer, had been his hero as a youngster.

Nevertheless the status of Sibson and Shutt changed completely on 25 February at Digbeth Civic Hall. A huge headline in the Boxing News read "Sibbo gets it done in 59 Secs", which just about sums up the destruction vested on opponent Gareth *Tashy* Jones by Tony's left hooks to his head and body. Although Jones had suffered a shock first round defeat previously he had been thought of as a bit of a prospect and many thought this would be a defining fight for both boxers. Tony recalled his views on the build up and the fight itself. "He was coming up like me. Everyone was still talking about him and I saw it as an all-or-nothing fight for me. I just went out, said to myself, 'Right, this is it', and just gave it to him." Manager Gunns was interviewed afterwards and explained that he wanted to keep Sibson busy but not with top ten fighters, reminding everyone that his prospect was still only eighteen years of age. It was noticeable in the interview that Gunns mentioned "Experience is more important than money at the moment", suggesting that this may have been an issue which was beginning to be discussed. By now Tony's fan base of loud and loyal supporters was increasing rapidly with Birmingham and Wolverhampton fight fans joining the throng from Leicester. Sadly it was not such a pleasant night for Paul Shutt who was stopped in the sixth round of his fight.

Big time professional boxing returned to Leicester after a ten year absence with Dave Roden's promotion at De Montford

Hall on 24 March, a show which attracted 1,500 fans. There was almost disaster for Sibson, his army of fans, and the promoter when his scheduled opponent Paddy Doherty failed to arrive from Belfast. Previous victim Bonny McKenzie received an invite at four in the afternoon and made his way up from Wales with the daunting prospect of facing the unbeaten Sibson, on his own turf and army of fans. Tony's fans wearing *Sibbo* tee-shirts and carrying banners gave their hero a huge ovation as he entered the ring. Sibson stormed out of the blocks and had McKenzie reeling before he fell to the canvas in round two. McKenzie toppled again in the sixth and was stopped on a cut eye in the next round. Despite the success, manager Gunns remained cautious. He remarked "Tony can box much better, mind you McKenzie did spoil a lot and didn't make things easy for him." To add to the occasion, Mickey Bell won again with a third round stoppage.

Sibson was now ranked eighth in Britain and manager Gunns stuck to his programme in having Tony out again on 7 April at Dudley Town Hall. When planned opponent Winston Cousins drew out, in stepped former light-heavyweight Steve Walker. Walker would have been more suited to the modern day super-middleweight division as his weight hovered around 12 stones. He only had four wins from twenty fights but one of those had been for the Midlands Area light-heavyweight championship. Sibson controlled the fight from beginning to end but it was a good enough workout for the young prospect. Looking back Tony demonstrated that he was not as naive as some people may have thought because he remembered his thoughts after the fight. "I looked at Steve Walker and his face. It was like looking into a history book. It wasn't like he was beat up or anything, but he was what boxers had been for years, probably for centuries. He knew what it was all for and he was there getting a few quid. He was a substitute again. He was using boxing as much as boxing was using him. I met him after the fight with his wife. He was a really nice man, a gentleman."

It was off to the famous old Liverpool Stadium on 21 April to fight former foe, Welshman Tony Burnett. This was a memorable experience for Sibson. "I love Liverpool. It was a big, big stadium, loads of character in the place. The dressing rooms were old, dated. It was like one of them old Rocky films, dated you know. You could smell the leather, the history of the place. All of the history you could feel it in them old changing rooms. I wished I'd been promoted in Liverpool at some time you know."

It looked like there would be another early win for the Leicester man. Burnett fell from a right hand in the second, and took a count of eight when down again in the fourth. However Burnett refused to wilt and fought back throwing a succession of body shots which slowed Sibson down. He was still throwing punches when the final bell rang and both boxers received a standing ovation as *nobbins* flew into the ring. This was an outstanding performance from Sibson with Liverpool promoter Manny Goodall telling Carl Gunns that he wanted him back as soon as possible as he believed he had never seen a youngster with so much talent. Gunns reported that in addition to his purse Sibson got £26 off the *nobbins* and that money had been "flying everywhere". Tony's manager had never seen Tony fight so well, even the referee joined in the acclaim telling Sibson that if he carried on boxing in a similar manner he would go right to the top. Sibson had this to say about his opponent "Tony Burnett was a tough, hard man. I knocked seven bells out of him and he just kept coming in and taking it. He made me look like a world champion. He must have been built of iron. I put my combinations together and hit him with everything, and I just couldn't put him away. He had so much bottle, he was untrue. He had black eyes and was banged up, but he knew just what to do and how to survive. We got nobbins, but I didn't deserve a penny of it. I was enjoying myself because it was like hitting the bag. I felt like I was showing off. He lived for fighting. Afterwards he was all banged up and he said to me 'Good fight'. I couldn't believe it. I thought to myself 'He enjoyed that!'" John Moores the Littlewoods Pools mogul invited both boxers on to the pitch before an Everton versus Newcastle game, the first football match the young Sibson had ever been to. They were presented with cheques for £100 each.

Sibson faced his first overseas opponent at De Montford Hall on 27 April. In the opposite corner from Zaire, although based in Luxembourg, was Sonny Kamunga. Tony boxed competently enough and was never in any trouble, although he suffered damage to his nose from a right hand in the fifth. Mickey Bell meantime had to settle for a disputed draw in his fight.

Sibson's progress was starting to transcend his popularity in the insular world of professional boxing. The Leicester Mercury had now put him forward with other sporting stars as a candidate for the Leicestershire Sports Personality of the Year. Nominated alongside him was Steven Sims the young Leicester City footballer who had already been capped twice at under 21 level for England.

As the natural summer boxing recess approached, Tony's run of fights stopped and it would be natural to claim that he enjoyed a well earned rest. However this was not entirely the case. As a young lad of nineteen he did what was perhaps natural. "I was drifting out of boxing. I was getting down the town. I was drinking, having fun, getting into clubs, oh you know what it's like. I was finding my feet in life and was in with a right crowd of nut-cases. My dad really let me have it. He said 'You could go somewhere'. I said 'Where?' He said 'Think of all the money you could earn'. He wasn't thinking about winning the championship, just about getting a few quid. But I listened to him."

It was not until an invitation to spar with Alan Minter in September that Sibson eventually got his mind back round to fighting. Minter was preparing for his defence of the European middleweight title in France against Gratien Tonna. Carl Gunns was contacted by Minter's manager Doug Bidwell and arrangements were made for Tony to go down to London for three days sparring at the Thomas à Beckett gym. Sibson was to spar four rounds each day, being paid £10 a round. When the Leicester contingent, including twenty fans who had taken time off work, turned up at the gym they saw that the place was full and the media were out in force. Carl and Tony were immediately on their guard being apprehensive that Tony was there as a *whipping boy*. Minter did catch Tony with an elbow during one session causing a nosebleed, but Tony recalls that he handled Minter pretty well, and perhaps that's why his services were dispensed with after a couple of days!

Sibson had his first fight in almost six months at Wolverhampton Civic Hall on 18 October, and the ring rust showed. Coming in very light at 01st 2lb he fought sluggishly against former British welterweight champion Pat Thomas, a late replacement for his brother Carl. Thomas had appeared to be on the slide, however, it's worth observing that he would go on to win and successfully defend the British light-middleweight crown. Thomas smothered much of Sibson's work although the Leicester favourite would get through with bursts of left hooks. At the end of eight rounds the referee brought Sibson's run of victories to an end when he raised both boxers' arms and declared the fight a draw, much to the surprise of most at ringside. Sibson recalled "Thomas was a slippery fighter, holding on all the way through, not allowing me to do anything. I won the fight. I didn't know my trade then, but I still won the fight. The only thing I regret is that he butted me – I don't think he meant it – in the last round and I got a cut eyebrow. That was an old scar from when I gave my mam some lip when we were walking back from Woolworth's and she was pushing the pushchair. She gave me a clip on the back of the head and I ran between two cars and a great fat kid ran over me on his bike!"

At the Gala Baths in West Bromwich Sibson got back on to winning ways with a clear points win over Wayne Bennett another Welshman. This 8 November bout was again a learning fight for Sibson against an opponent who had beaten Eddie Burke in his last contest. The Scotsman Burke was a rising star and was listed just below Sibson in the rankings. Bennett had fought other good quality fighters and it's surprising that this would prove to be his second last contest. Bennett tried to fight at long range but Sibson's aggression carried the day.

His last fight of the year was a tough one against the experienced Oscar Angus. The Londoner had mixed with quality middleweights having travelled the distance twice with former British champion Kevin Finnegan who had just lost his title to Alan Minter. Their fight at Wolverhampton Civic Hall on 30 November proved just how far the nineteen year old Sibson had come. He marched through Angus and in the sixth round he was taken to pieces and battered with hooks and uppercuts. At the end of that session Angus's manager George Francis pulled him out much to the annoyance of the proud southerner. Carl Gunns believed Sibson only performed at 75% of the level he had in his previous fight and thought he was eighteen months away from challenging for the British title. The packed crowd thought otherwise.

Towards the end of the year Midlands promoter Ron Gray, manager Johnny Griffin and Carl Gunns were stirring up a *war of words* over a proposed battle between Sibson and his former amateur gym mate, Dougie Ralston. Gray and Griffin both thought that it'd be a money spinner capable of selling out the De Montford Hall within days. On the other hand Gunns was suggesting that Tony had *bigger fish to fry* in that he was looking to direct him towards a British title challenge. The twenty-eight year old Ralston may have been eyeing up a lucrative payday before he was much older and there could have been little doubt that the fight would have been a sell-out.

Tony was becoming a real celebrity around Leicester, an example of which came from a story remembered fondly by his brother Troy. "When Tony got home from work we used to go a five mile training run from our house. At the end of the run we used to speed up along Gleneagles Avenue and finish at Our Lady's Church. This was on a bus route and the bus drivers started to recognise us, because I had *Tony Sibson* printed on the back of my tee-shirt, and they realised we were racing them along the street. They drivers joined in the race and even though there were bus stops along the Avenue, they didn't stop at them, just to try to win the race. The passengers would get off at the church in groups and talk to us when we finished. Even the Canon from the church came out. One or two complained that they missed their stop, but everybody just laughed!"

It had been another excellent year in the ring for Sibson and to outsider's it must have seemed that he was thriving on his success. Nothing could have been further from the truth. He was starting to look around at the packed halls he was fighting in, filled primarily with his supporters, and wondering why he was not earning more. He would speak to other boxers at these shows and learn how much they were getting in comparison to him. The young nineteen year old speculated at how much the promoters were taking in on ticket sales and felt that his manager should have been more forceful in his negotiations with them with regard to purse money. Having a bigger impact on Sibson was the fact that, for him, the enjoyment he had been experiencing from fighting was gradually disappearing. The camaraderie he had relished, and needed, backstage in his early fights from his former Belgrave club mates had gone. He was now usually *top of the bill* and the others were no longer appearing with him.

Becoming a well known face around Leicester, and the attention he was getting from people outwith his circle of

friends and relatives was becoming painful for the excruciatingly shy Sibson. He knew he blushed when strangers spoke to
him and that fact alone made his problem seem worse. To a
young man, who should have been out enjoying himself, he was
starting to question the wisdom of choosing boxing as a career
path. The irony of it all, of course, was that it was his success
that was causing all the problems!

CHAPTER 4

Disaster!

The young, increasingly disillusioned Sibson, was now aboard a runaway train and he couldn't get off. Fights were arranged, friends were wishing him well, tickets were being bought and the Belgrave trainers were pushing him on to greater heights. They seemed to be living their boxing ambitions through him and he simply couldn't, or wouldn't, let them down.

It was back into action at Wolverhampton Civic Hall on 23 January with Scottish light-middleweight champion, John Smith, in the opposite corner. Smith was a *have gloves will travel* sort of fighter who'd engaged in sixty-one contests, winning only twenty-three prior to meeting Sibson. He did however usually last the distance, and as Tony had said previously about Steve Walker, he knew what his job was. Towards the end of the fourth round Sibson caught him with a left hook putting him down. A similar punch in the next round led to the referee counting the Scotsman out. "That was a fight I enjoyed – John Smith. I hit him clean with a left hook. It was there before I knew it. But I remember having expected more from him." Sibson's recollection demonstrated the gym work and sparring had honed his left hook to perfection.

Sibson's fame was extending beyond the Midlands and in their edition of 24 February, the Boxing News devoted their entire centre pages to a feature on him. It was becoming clear that he was recognised as a potential future champion and suggestions were being made that he needed now to appear in a London ring. Manager Gunns though made the subtle point that while he was prepared to travel to the capital he would not put his young star at risk against *last minute replacements*. The article also reported that Tony was augmenting his boxing training by working out at the Healthland Centre in Leicester managed by Dave Boorman, and also training there at the time was top level 400 metres runner David Jenkins. It was obvious that, considering the heavy work he was doing on the building sites and this additional programme at the Healthland Centre, he was getting physically stronger, a factor which wouldn't have been happy news for future opponents.

Sibson's views on his boxing career around this time are revealing. "I wanted to win, you know. You could read between the lines, everything is getting big. In the beginning it was about money but I wasn't getting my pound of flesh. I never thought about winning the British title, I knew what it was but it wasn't in my mind. It wasn't there at the time. If you'd said Midlands Area title, well, I didn't look that far ahead. A deposit for a house that's all I wanted." From this statement Tony had two obvious aims. To keep winning, and to earn well. Titles were an afterthought.

As the date of his next fight on 6 March approached a belief was growing that Leicester and the Midlands in general had found a new boxing superstar. Ranked number seven and having the longest unbeaten run in British boxing, Sibson had his first ten round contest against a man rated two positions higher in the shape of Errol McKenzie. At the weigh-in Sibson came in at

11st 10.5lb, two and a half pounds over the contracted limit. McKenzie's manager demanded that he either lost the extra poundage or forfeit £25. Sibson was not about to throw away hard cash and set about losing the weight. Tony remembered "I tried running it off, but I was wearing cowboy boots and tight jeans, dressed up like a lead guitarist. I tried running round the block, but it was ridiculous. I thought 'stuff this, I can't do it' and I just dived into a sauna." He managed to sweat off two pounds and this was accepted by the opposition camp.

The Welshman had won eleven of fourteen bouts and was well respected. However the expectant crowd at Wolverhampton Civic Hall saw a devastating performance from their local hero. McKenzie tried to trade with Sibson towards the end of the first and was caught with a right hand followed by a left hook. He was lucky to hear the bell while still on his feet. Early in the next, a short right and a left bounced McKenzie off the canvas and as the end of the round approached another right floored him leaving him to be counted out by the referee. Afterwards McKenzie's manager Mac Williams said "The last fighter Sibson kayoed, John Smith, said it was like the lights had been turned out and that's what Errol said to me afterwards. Is Sibson good? Listen, you've got to be good to kayo McKenzie. No one's ever done it before. Carl Gunns added "His last four fights have seen a terrific improvement. We know he's hitting much harder than he's ever done before. We can feel it on the bag."

This was an extremely busy and demanding period for Carl Gunns, who, we should remember, was still only thirty-two years old and now had another six fighters under his wing. The managers of potential opponents knew all about Sibson. What's more, he had the reputation of being a *banger*. He had just beaten a man rated number five in the country, but was still only approaching his twentieth birthday. Not having been in the role long, Gunns didn't have time to forge the links and contacts necessary to ensure that Tony's career continued to progress as smoothly as it had done up until then. On the one hand he had Midlands promoters like Ron Gray and Dave Roden anxious to have Tony on their shows simply because he was a great ticket seller. Coupled with this though was a natural tendency by the promoters to have lower level opponents for him knowing that they would demand smaller purses. The other alternative course of action and one which must have occupied Gunns' mind was to line up higher quality opposition in preparation for future championship battles. That course of action would necessitate taking him out of his Midlands fan base, working with promoters Gunns didn't know well, and for money which might not be any higher than what he was getting in the meantime. The current British champion was Alan Minter with leading contenders being Kevin Finnegan, Frank Lucas, Bunny Sterling and Sibson.

Sibson's next two fights appear to suggest that Gunns took the former route. 31 March was the eve of the Grand National and Tony turned up once more at Liverpool Stadium to face Ghanaian Mac Nicholson. Nicholson was having his first fight in Britain having won eleven out of his last twelve in Ghana and proved to made of stern stuff. He stung Sibson with a solid left hook in the first thirty seconds and the Leicester boxer was more cautious afterwards. In the seventh round, Nicholson, bleeding from the nose and his right eye, was trapped in his own corner and being systematically broken down when the referee intervened to rescue him.

The following day promoter Ron Gray and manager Gunns were talking up a fight with highly rated Southampton middleweight Jan Magdziarz. Gray felt this fight could be a decider to find a challenger for the British title. Gray told the Leicester Mercury "I can't see how the authorities can refuse, for both men have tremendous records." Magdziarz's manager Jack Bishop commented on his own fighter saying "Nobody in the division wants to know him, apart from Sibson" which was fair comment given that he had already beaten both Minter and top contender Frankie Lucas.

There was not much of a rest for Sibson after his Mersey excursion because four days later he appeared as a late substitute at Wolverhampton Civic Hall to save promoter Ron Gray's bacon. He faced old foe Steve Walker in a fight that started one minute after midnight to comply with the Board of Control's rule that four clear days must elapse between fights. Sibson understandably looked jaded but he began to get to Walker in the fourth and in the next round finished it with short right and left hooks to the head and body. Tony did not want this fight. "I had already fought Steve, and I liked him anyway, as a person, he was a good man. I respected him as a person, and I didn't want that fight. I didn't want to go through that process, I didn't enjoy that at all. It just shows how ruthless managers and matchmakers are. They didn't care about it, but I did."

By the middle of April Carl Gunns' continuing dilemma about how to progress Sibson's career took another turn when he agreed to a fight at the Royal Albert Hall in London on a Mike Barrett promotion. His planned opponent was the very capable Billy Knight who had recently moved up to light-heavyweight, necessitating the match being made at 12st.

Four hundred Leicester fans made their way to London for the big fight, but Carl Gunns' worst fears materialised when the scheduled opponent pulled out, being replaced by previous victim Mac Nicholson. Sibson took out his annoyance on the unlucky Ghanaian pummelling him relentlessly for the one and a half minutes the fight lasted. The victory did however impress the hard-bitten London fight crowd and a wider television audience with Sibson appearing on the BBC for the first time. Commentator Harry Carpenter seemed amazed by Tony's long red trunks and his vociferous Leicester support when they started up with the "Sibbo, Sibbo" football chant.

Gunns told the press afterwards "Tony is definitely not one of those fighters who will prop up an opponent for a few rounds just for the hell of it. His aim is to put them away as quickly as possible no matter who they are. He likes it that way and that is what the crowd come to see." Gunns added that Sibson's next fight would be the anticipated *decider* against Magdziarz the following month, in Leicester.

The express train which was Sibson's career up until now was headed for an unexpected derailment. Occasionally people are faced with a decision and afterwards, when that decision has turned into a disaster, they ask themselves how they could have avoided it. That must surely have been on Carl Gunns' mind in the days, weeks and even years after Tony's next fight. On another big Leicester show at the De Montford Hall on 23 May he was matched with Zambian light-heavyweight Lotte Mwale after original opponent Magdziarz pulled out. Mwale then based in London was training under the experienced eye of George Francis. Francis knew what to expect from Sibson as he had handled Oscar Angus in his fight with Tony six months previously. It would later come to light that the vastly experienced Francis knew that Tony was neither big enough nor good enough at that time to handle Mwale and Mickey Duff, who worked closely with Francis, had tried to get the fight put off. The bout was made at 12st 2lb.

Mwale had won all six of his professional contests, five by way of knockout. The trade paper recognised this with the Boxing News headline stating *Mwale Spells Danger for Sibson.* It is likely that Carl Gunns did not know too much about Mwale when the match was made. There were reports that he'd won 274 of 277 amateur contests, winning five gold medals in various tournaments. After only a handful of professional fights he was already rated number five in the Commonwealth light-heavyweight rankings. Gunns of course was not to know that Mwale had an impressive future ahead of him as both a world class fighter, with a world class punch. It is easy now to look back and criticise Sibson's manager, but we have to put ourselves back into his shoes at that time. Tony was dealing comfortably with anyone put in front of him, knocking most out. He had fought light-heavyweights before and handled them with ease. Mac Nicholson for instance had a relatively similar background to Mwale, and perhaps Gunns simply saw the Zambian as another slight step-up in competition. Gunns would in the future get upset when people commented on the apparent weight discrepancy pointing out that he insisted on the match being made well below the light-heavyweight limit and at the weigh-in there wasn't much difference between them. How much this fight, and its conclusion, disturbed Gunns was demonstrated years afterwards when he still felt the need to write a personal letter to the Boxing News defending his position.

Tony looked on this fight the way he did all the others up until then. His attitude was crystal clear. He did the work, turned up on the night and was paid for his efforts. His family and friends once again turned out in their droves and packed the local venue to the rafters. The now familiar chants were bellowed out and the *Sibbo* tee shirts were plentiful. It seemed that it was just another night, and another win, along the road.

Mwale came out in the first looking confident and after only two and a half minutes, moved Sibson into the ropes, slid in a couple of jabs and blasted over a right hand which landed flush on Tony's chin. The young starlet was unconscious before he hit the ground. Not many of us have suffered a clean knockout from a punch or anything else for that matter, and it's hard to imagine what it feels like if you haven't experienced it. Sibson is able to tell us how it affected him. "I was dead. Three minutes I was dead for. That's a long time. I was laying into him and the next minute I'm dead. Full stop. It was awful. It's happened once and that's all I ever want it to happen." Tony's friend Mickey Bell remembered the night well. "I was sitting in the crowd and the place was buzzing. They were all screaming and shouting. I was watching the ring and Tony came out looking all right. Then 'bang' he was out. I can remember the silence, nobody could believe it. We were all shocked. I went back to the Belgrave

Working Mens Club afterwards and later Tony came in. We all tried to support him."

Mwale would go on fighting until 1994 and ended with a career record of forty-four wins from fifty-three fights. The important statistic being that thirty-four of his wins came through knockouts. He would go on to fight some of best boxers in the world at light-heavyweight.

This was a massive shock for young Sibson and his Leicester fans. Mwale's coach George Francis said it was the cleanest knockout he had ever seen in thirty-years in the game. Carl Gunns admitted it was a colossal mistake taking on Mwale but this error of judgement had long term effects on Sibson and he explained why. "When I came to, I lay there thinking 'Jesus Christ, I'm here and wearing the shorts my Auntie Pearl made me.' At that time I was living in a flat in Leicester and my neighbours didn't know what I did. But the next night, there I am, flat on my back all over the back page of the Mercury. I had a day off work and went to see the doctor. No way was I boxing to get hurt. I was sticking at it because I was winning and I was having a good time and so was everybody else. I didn't have any illusions that I was anybody important. I used to go to the gym two or maybe three times a week and do a Sunday morning if the others were going to be there and that was it. I was working on the site and was fit, but I was just a kid. Nobody told me I was stepping out of my depth. Nobody told me who I was fighting. I trusted people. And it was a mismatch from the start. I can accept that a man's better than me, but I can't accept having my trousers down. I didn't know what to think about Carl. Maybe he had been conned or intimidated. Maybe he was scared to say no. Carl said afterwards it was his fault, but it was me with my picture in the papers on my back. I'd sold £16,000 worth of tickets in my own town all for that. To be done over like that. I'm a proud man and I come from good people and none of us deserved that. I had a brain scan done myself to make sure I was OK because I've always known the sort of things that can happen. Then I thought 'Right the party's over. This has been an apprenticeship – and it's finished with.'"

Almost forty-five years later Tony recalled a relatively minor incident from the day after the fight which summoned up just how important close friends, and their sincerity, meant to him. "Tom Amoroso, was a Leicester kid. When we were kids he was a hard case. When he was coming down the street you ran round the corner. Him and his family were hard cases. They were Italians they couldn't speak good English. You would avoid them. You would get a slap off them, you know what I mean? And Tom came across the road to me and said, 'Don't you worry about anything, you done us all proud'. He knew what was needed, I've never forgot that, I get emotional thinking about it even today."

Gunns and Sibson wanted another fight, and a win, before the summer recess. With clean knockouts like this there can be a danger that the fighter becomes *gun shy*, so it's important to restore his confidence. His next fight for Ron Gray at Wolverhampton on 29 June was designed to do just that. This time he was facing Mancunian light-heavyweight Danny McLoughlin.

McLoughlin had won eight of sixteen fights and in January had drawn with Tony's pal, Steve Fenton. It was probably the ideal fight at the time and it served its purpose with Sibson stopping McLoughlin with a rib bending left hook in the third round. After the contest Gunns mentioned this would be Tony's last fight at light-heavyweight. The manager added that he was having difficulty getting matches with middleweights in Britain due to Sibson's fearsome reputation and he might have to look elsewhere if they didn't materialise. Gunns also asserted that the fight had swept away the psychological scars left by Mwale but this was not how Sibson saw it. "No, there weren't any scars. Not that kind anyway. I'd been educated, not psychologically upset, not in terms of being afraid to fight."

Sibson appeared at a new venue for him on 18 July at the Theatre Club in Wakefield. He was up against former victim, Bonny McKenzie. This was his third meeting with the Welshman who'd been stopped in both previous occasions in the seventh round. This time McKenzie went the full distance although he was down four times in the sixth and seventh rounds against a slightly jaded Sibson who seemed to rely solely on his left hooks.

Manager Gunns had added another handful of boxers to his ever increasing stable over the summer, and when he lined Sibson up to fight on Mickey Duff's inaugural promotion at Wembley Conference Centre against unbeaten Keith Bussey it was clear he was intent on pushing him towards a British title fight. Bussey was unbeaten in seventeen fights, stopping former Belgrave teammate Paul Shutt last time out. He had beaten a long list of previous Sibson opponents including Burnett, Pickard, Breen, Winfield, McHugh with Tashy Jones managing to force the Londoner to a draw. In many ways this was an eliminator between two of the country's star youngsters at middleweight and there can be little doubt that another defeat for Sibson after the Mwale disaster could have been an irrevocable set-back.

As it happened Sibson got to Bussey in the last round bombarding him with right and left hooks before the Camberwell lad pulled Tony down with him as he collapsed to the floor. The referee counted to eight but realised that Bussey was in no position to continue and called it off. There was added satisfaction for the Leicester man, George Francis, who had been with Mwale, was in Bussey's corner. But it had not all been plain sailing for the Midlander. He'd been unusually cautious and early on was taking solid right hands as he moved forward, much as he did when losing to Mwale. He did have Bussey over twice in the early rounds but he bounced up so quickly the referee didn't have time to count. The Boxing News report on the fight might have been a bit harsh on Sibson with their criticism because he was in with a quality opponent and perhaps it was appropriate tactics to be a bit more tentative when he moved in to attack. What was impressive was how Sibson demolished his opponent at the end. To add to the perceived awkwardness of the performance Auntie Pearl's trunks took a pounding, ripping up at the rear early on! Within a year Bussey's career was over and can anyone say with certainty that a Sibson defeat would not have had the same outcome?

There were growing problems in the Sibson camp. Following the Mwale defeat, he had beaten all those put in front of him, and the Bussey victory had been important, but the fast, attacking, powerful punching Sibson from his earlier fights had disappeared. Either Sibson was maturing as a fighter and learning to take his time, or the right hand from Mwale had taken away a lot of his youthful confidence. There is another possibility and this can be found in the circumstances leading up to his next fight, only four weeks after the Bussey win. He had moved out the flat he had been sharing. "I just left everything there. All my belongings, everything. I just got out and thought 'Jesus, I need to be earning.'" He contacted his manager and told him he wanted a fight – any fight. They were offered Eddie Smith at the Royal Albert Hall on 24 October and Tony overruled Gunns who wanted to turn it down.

Smith had squeezed in twenty-three fights in his two years as a pro, winning eighteen. He was certainly *no mug* and Tony should have been prepared for a tough fight. However he went on holiday to Corfu and came back *fat as a pig and broke.* Unknown to the boxing public, Sibson would later claim he lost around nine pounds in the week before the show and had lost four pounds in a sauna on the day of the fight. This effort, to make the contracted weight for the contest, must have left the Leicester boxer totally de-hydrated and unfit to take on any type of opponent never mind someone of Smith's capability. The fight as it turned out was close with Smith taking a close points decision but it was, on Sibson's own admission, an embarrassment. Tony was hurt from body shots and forced to hold on repeatedly. His punches looked weak and Smith's corner, sensing this, exhorted him to throw more right hands. In the later rounds the weight weakened Sibson could do nothing but soak up hurtful hooks to the body, although he did mount a revival in the last session. The Boxing News asked rhetorically if Sibson simply couldn't make the middleweight limit anymore or whether he was slacking in his training. Sibson described how he felt during the fight which demonstrated how out of condition he really was. "I wouldn't give in because I knew people out there were looking out for me. I would have died rather than give in. That's the stupid attitude you've got when you're young. But I can remember being on my stool not being able to breathe. I had a burning sensation in my chest, I thought I was going to have a heart attack. But it was only because I wasn't fit, because I'd dehydrated and everything. Afterwards I was completely exhausted. I couldn't take deep breaths, yet I was gasping for breath and it was hurting so badly. Eddie Smith outfought me, he was like Joe Frazier, never stopped. I was down in the dressing room at the Albert Hall and there was just me and a mate. He said, 'look around you, where are they all now?'. He didn't mean my friends, the people who had come down from Leicester just to watch the fight, but the people who were involved in boxing, who controlled fighters. When you're a winner you have everyone in your dressing room. All the promoters feeding up on you, saying 'son, son, son.' That's always annoyed me. My dad is the only man in the world who is entitled to call me 'son'."

The following week Carl Gunns contacted the Boxing News to dispute the weight loss story. He said that there must have been a misunderstanding and that Sibson only lost nine pounds in two weeks and that his boxers never used saunas to lose extra poundage. Whatever the reality of the situation was, Sibson had his last fight of the year two weeks later and his official weight was given as 11st 5.5lb.

His opponent at the Wembley Arena was Frenchman Gerard Nosley. Once again, Gunns' previous concerns about fighting in London and opponents being switched at the last minute came to fruition. The scheduled opponent had been Dino Del Cid, but in came Nosley who was a southpaw and not what the Sibson camp had been anticipating. Again Tony looked hesitant and over-cautious but got the job done, halting the Frenchman in the seventh.

Another year came to an end, with mixed results. It had got off to a flier and ended with a big win over Bussey, but the Mwale defeat was a disaster and the performances against Eddie Smith and Nosley showed a definite decline. Sibson was not a happy lad. If it had been possible he would have walked away from boxing, at least for a time, due to all the previous concerns that were now having a tangible effect on his life. Tony's sister Karen believes that although there were other pressures on him to keep boxing, the most significant was the fact that he couldn't have faced his dad, Keith, with the news. His father had always encouraged his son's boxing career, and there'd been occasions when a strong word in Tony's young ear had kept him on the *straight and narrow*. Training had become a chore, he was indulging in his favourite pastime of eating all the wrong food at the wrong times, and his heart just wasn't in it.

CHAPTER 5

British Champion

The year started with Sibson at a low ebb and seriously doubting he had a future in boxing. It's hard to imagine someone with a future looking so bright, with the prestige and financial rewards on offer, contemplating giving it all up. He didn't mind the actual fighting, nor for that matter the training, but everything else, particularly the constant attention, was causing him sleepless nights. The following set of circumstances is an example of the type of thing which really unsettled him.

In early January Sibson learned, from a television broadcast, that his next fight in less than seven days time would be a challenge to Bunny Johnson for the British title at *light-heavyweight* on a Ron Gray promotion in Wolverhampton. He was furious and discovered that when a scheduled fight for Johnson had fallen through, promoter Ron Gray and Tony's manager Carl Gunns agreed terms for a contest without his knowledge. When Tony put his foot down telling Carl that he wouldn't fight, Gray made a special trip to Leicester in an effort resolve matters. The meeting did not go well! Sibson recalled what happened. "I heard Ron tell Carl 'You're his manager, tell him he's fighting.' Carl came in and said 'I'm your manager, and you're fighting.' I said 'You get stuffed' or something like that. It went on for a while, then Ron and the bloke he had come over with left. I knew I wasn't a light-heavyweight and Bunny

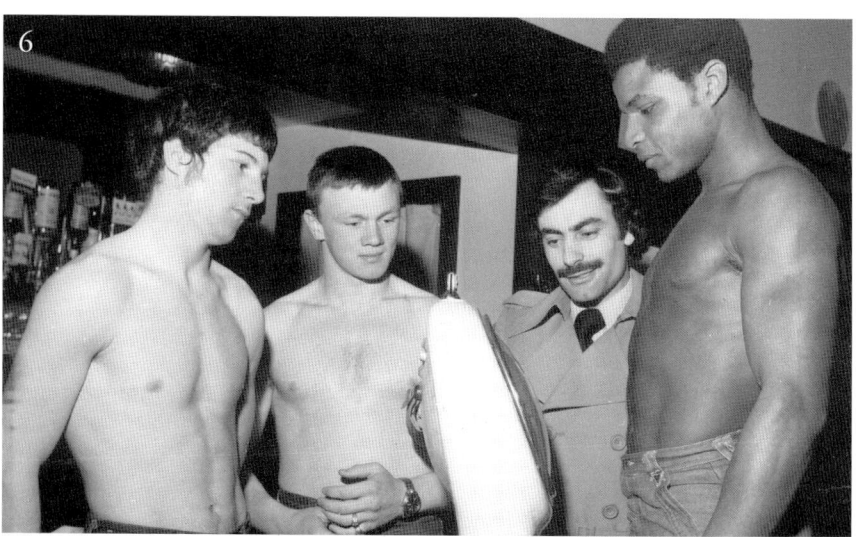

Previous page: 1: Back court in Bardolph Street, Tony, Karen, Craig and Troy Sibson. *2:* The young Sibbo. *3:* Sibson – the hod carrier. *4:* First Job in Parkers Abbattoir. *This page: 5:* Tony, George Biddles and Carl Gunns signing manager's contract. *6:* Mickey Bell, Tony and Carl Gunns watch Romel Ambrose check his weight.

7: Tony with proud mum after beating Lucas for British title.
8: Sibson lands a left hook on James Waire – 22 January 1980.
Photograph by kind permission of Action Images.

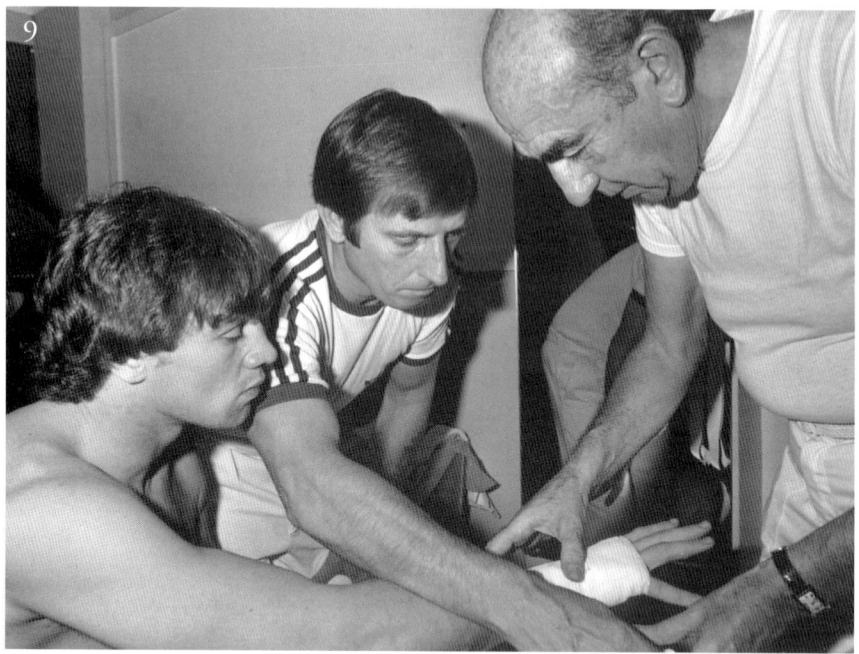

This page: 9: Tony, Ken Squires and Sam Burns examine his bandages. *10:* Referee moves in to pull Sibson back after stopping Minter – 15 September 1981. Photograph by kind permission of Action Images.

Johnson had been heavyweight champion as well. They said to me 'He's an old man, Tony, you can take him.' But what if I had, what then? I just wasn't a light-heavyweight."

It was back to Wolverhampton Civic Hall on 5 March for his first fight in 1979 against the only British fighter to have beaten him so far, Eddie Smith. This was a bout which had to take place before Sibson could progress to a British title challenge but it was almost cancelled because Tony was unwell a week before the fight. "I was in bed and I wanted to pull out, but people were saying I'd never get a fight again if I did, and I thought I had to go through with it. I know now it was a load of rubbish, but I didn't know then."

Smith had stopped Chris Lawson in January, his only fight since winning at the Royal Albert Hall and he'd moved up the rankings to now being only two places behind Sibson. The problems Tony faced prior to their previous fight were not widely known and it was important to gain revenge over Smith to restore the faith his supporters had in him. If he had pulled out the rumours would have started and it's likely he could have slipped out of title contention for the foreseeable future.

Sibson won a close fight thanks to the brisk start he made, but as the fight wore on Smith made a comeback and by the end of the ten rounds appeared to be getting on top. The effects of the flu were tiring Sibson out as the fight progressed and he was left bleeding from the nose at the bell. Tony had great respect for Smith and his fellow boxers and made some harsh comments on the fight game. "Eddie Smith, I love that person. I'll always think of him fondly and he'll think of me, I know he will. They can exploit you and take your money away from you, but when two people get in the ring and give each other everything they've got, it's hard to put into words how you feel for a person who can do that. We didn't mean harm to each other. We were both in a rat race, we were both in the end getting ripped off. We're all brothers, fighters, black, white, red whatever you are."

This had been a tough fight for Sibson and he explained some of the feelings he'd experienced during the contest. "You know what made me win the second fight? Fear of feeling like I did in the first one, and because one of the lads in my corner said to me, 'Think of your granddad, think of your grandad'. It was about the seventh round and I was sold out. He's walking through me again and he's non-stop motion, I'm back-pedalling. Then somebody said that. I thought 'Oh, don't do that to me, don't lay that one on me. 'I'm so knackered I can't give it. I could hear them in the gallery saying, 'Come on Tony, come on.' I was thinking 'I've had enough.' I can hear my dad in the crowd, and the nightmare of the first fight came back to me. I was saying to myself, 'Come on, you don't want to feel like you did the first time, get him out of there.' I was scaring myself to dig deep into my body, to find out what was there and to stop myself looking for an excuse to stop. We just stood toe-to-toe. I boxed southpaw sometimes, but it was just a motion. Just pushing it out. I couldn't have knocked a fly over and I didn't think he could. We'd both given our best. Eddie Smith could have been a champion and worthy of it." What an insight into a boxers mentality during a big fight and how interesting it is to consider if *home* advantage can effect a sportsman's performance?

This fight once again focussed Sibson's attention on the financial side of the business. "I looked around and it was my fans that were filling the place. Ron Gray had a licence to print money when he was promoting Tony Sibson. Wolverhampton would have been filled every week if I had been fighting. I don't feel bitter towards anybody now, it's all so long ago." It's not difficult to understand where the young Sibson was coming from but he might not have fully appreciated how much money a promoter was required to outlay against ticket sales. Ron Gray would have had to pay for the hire of the hall, the cost of officials, purses for other boxers on the card, and a whole host of incidental expenses.

Unknown at the time to Tony or Carl Gunns was the fact that promoter Mike Barrett was having trouble finding a *top of the bill* fight for his one hundredth promotion at the Royal Albert Hall. The British middleweight title was in disarray following Alan Minter's abdication the previous autumn and leading contender Frankie Lucas was matched controversially with Bunny Sterling, with the winner to meet Kevin Finnegan. That fight fell through when Sterling pulled out and Barrett had replaced him with Finnegan for his big show on 10 April. Disaster struck when Finnegan too pulled out with the flu. Meanwhile up in the Midlands a disillusioned Sibson was preparing to meet Michel Stini of Belgium on a Ron Gray show in Leicester. Then Mike Barrett came along with an offer they couldn't refuse. At the same time as the fight was being arranged Barrett and his partner Mickey Duff covered their back in case of an upset by securing options on Sibson's first two defences. This was what Tony had feared. "I wasn't a great reader, and the contracts were complicated for both Carl and me. I didn't know what people wrote to me. Carl dealt with Mike Barrett and I just sat in the background. I said to Carl, 'If I beat Frankie Lucas, we've got a chance of making some money. Whatever you do, don't sign us away. We've got to stay freelance and get the best pay-day.' Carl never said that he had, but he was sheepish. You could sense something was wrong. I didn't realise, but I signed away my defences for £3,500 for each fight. Two defences. One against Kevin Finnegan."

As you would expect with a late substitute coming in for a British title challenge, Tony was a clear underdog with very few people out with his own family and friends plus his loyal supporters thinking he could win. The Boxing News predicted that his only chance was to stop the injury prone Lucas on cut eyes, but felt that a late stoppage for the Croydon southpaw was the most likely outcome.

Lucas was an extremely tough customer who, although having only fifteen fights in almost five years as a professional, had faced top quality opposition from the word go. He had already fought for the British title when he was stopped in the eleventh round by Kevin Finnegan, but had then went to Turin and knocked out the Italian star Jacopucci in the second round. His management team then took him out to Zambia to face the tough local Chisanda Mutti and Lucas again upset the odds by stopping the favourite in the ninth round. His losing contests were usually as a result of injuries and he was not averse to a few *dirty tricks* in the ring. He was generally considered in the game to be a bit of an *animal*.

On the day of the fight the *out-of-towner* weighed in surprisingly light at 11st 3lb, and this was taken by some as further evidence that Sibson and his people were out of their depth. The bookmakers had Sibson as the 6-4 underdog. Everyone who knew Tony had travelled to London including, wheelchair bound, grandfather Wally, and they made their presence felt when Sibson made his way to the ringside behind Carl Gunns. Also in the crowd, along with regulars at the Sibson fan club based in the Gipsy Lane Hotel, was Swedish casino owner Klas Zell. Zell was a friend of landlord Barry Garrigan and had apparently followed Tony's career from his amateur days. It was estimated that around 1,000 fans travelled down from Leicestershire for the fight.

As the boxers came together mid-ring to receive their final instructions from referee Wally Thom, Lucas couldn't resist attempting to intimidate his young opponent by sticking his forehead into Sibson's face, but if he thought this had the desired effect he was very much mistaken. Sibson pushed him back, an action which required Thom to bring them together again to touch gloves. This gave Sibson a great deal of satisfaction. "When he started, I just grinned at him. All he did was set the match to the fuse. I could have been back on the pavements in Bardolph Street!"

Both fighters came out fired up and it was Sibson who landed first with a succession of left hooks. Lucas scored cleanly with a left uppercut and left hook from his southpaw stance and stood in mid ring shouting at Sibson in a show of aggression. The round was fought at a fierce pace, swinging one way then another and at the bell Lucas probably edged it with the cleaner punches. Tony's fans had bought £4,000 worth of tickets and the noise inside the Hall was deafening.

Lucas seemed to have calmed down in the second round and

scored regularly with right jabs. He looked confident as Sibson's attacks appeared to lack any effect. It's likely that the Croydon man had secured the first two rounds in a fight commentator Harry Carpenter thought wouldn't last the distance. The third started with Lucas on the front foot chasing Sibson around the ring with the Leicester fighter looking like his early fire had died down. Midway through the round, when coming out of a clinch Sibson could be seen speaking into Lucas's ear. When reminded of this years later Sibson could remember saying to Lucas "I'm hurting you now." In the latter half of the round Sibson was landing cleanly with left hooks and jabs which probably opened the cut above Lucas's eye and won him this stanza. Sibson commented later on the third round saying "It was a one-off. Two raw, aggressive maniacs. I'd certainly flipped my lid, I know that. It was raw, somehow more truthful. Being a textbook boxer is like being a solicitor. This was just straight-to-the-point, honest-to-God street fighting." Young manager Gunns, in the corner with Sibson, found himself in a unique and highly charged situation. The corner could see they were on the point of winning the British title and were struggling to remain calm, which unsettled Sibson.

It is worthwhile looking at the set-up in Sibson's corner. From time immemorial the Chief Second in charge of organising a boxer's corner has invariably been the trainer, the man who works with the fighter on a daily basis. When it gets to championship level an expert cut man may be introduced. Occasionally the manager, if he has an extensive background in boxing, may decide he also wants to make himself available. The Chief Second in Tony's corner was his manager Carl Gunns.

Gunns had adopted this role for many, if not all, of Sibson's fights. Also assisting Gunns were Les Anderson who was skilled in dealing with cuts, and Mick Gutteridge, a good friend to the fighter.. Neither of these men were Tony's trainer. That function was the domain of Jim Knight, Ken Squires and others at the Belgrave ABC. It would have been difficult for any of the corner men, although experienced boxing people, to provide relevant tactical advice to Sibson given that it's unlikely they'd know what the trainers had been working on in the build up to the fight. Knight, Squires and the rest at the Belgrave ABC didn't have professional licences at that time.

The fourth followed a similar pattern with Lucas winning the early exchanges and Sibson firing back later on. It was noticeable that Lucas was throwing a lot more body shots in an attempt to slow the youngster down, but Sibson seemed to be taking them well enough. In the next round the body shots from Lucas continued and now they were having an impact with Sibson trying to take a step back from the action in order to get his wind back. But just as it was beginning to look like Tony had shot his bolt, and with his back to the ropes, he unleashed a short left hook which landed flush on the older man's chin dropping him like a stone. He rose on unsteady legs looking towards his corner, but not really knowing where he was. Sibson tore in to finish it and Lucas was knocked down twice more. When he rose for the third time it was obvious he couldn't defend himself, and at two minutes and thirty-two seconds of the fifth round, a star was born. Britain and Leicester had a new middleweight champion.

Erstwhile trainer Ken Squires reckoned that events at ringside following this fight were the reason the Leicester contingent always believed that legendary BBC commentator Harry Carpenter had it in for Sibson. He recalled with a grin "When the fight finished the Leicester lot came to the front and tried to get into the ring with Tony. It was chaos. Somebody slapped Carpenter on the back of the head, and somebody else stood on his typewriter!"

There was little time to enjoy his success, because a month later, on 14 May at Wembley Conference Centre, Sibson was back in the ring for a ten rounder against American import Al Clay. Clay had won eight from thirteen contests and was fighting outside the States for the first time. He was an ideal opponent for the new British champion in that he didn't present any real danger but was capable of lasting a few rounds. It turned out to be a plodding sort of performance from Sibson and at one point the referee had to call for more action. Clay must have regretted the referee's intervention because seconds later it was all over, following a left hook from Sibson which flattened the visitor. Tony summed up his feelings when he said "It all felt ordinary again. I must admit I'm my own worst enemy sometimes, but I lost something with the Lucas fight." This view is understandable. Sometimes the excitement comes from the struggle to get to the top and once the pinnacle is reached it seems that everything thereafter is an anti-climax, it's not what's expected. Tony did concede that the money he received from Mickey Duff for the Clay fight was the amount agreed with Carl Gunns for a British title defence and not what he'd anticipated from a routine ten rounder.

An interesting situation existed as far as middleweight boxing in Britain was concerned. Although Sibson was the

British champion, Alan Minter, who had given up this title previously, was still the European champion and also considered to be the number one contender for the world crown. Kevin Finnegan, who should have fought Lucas for the British title, was the third ranked contender behind Minter in Europe, one in front of Tony. It's clear that Minter was being guided towards a world title shot with Finnegan still considered as the British champion in waiting. The top London promoters knew that the potential for big, money-earning fights within the middle-weight division involving Minter, Finnegan, Sibson and even Frank Lucas could keep the tills ringing for some time.

Another *marking time* fight for Sibson was arranged for 26 June back home in Leicester. Little did anyone know at the time that this would be Tony's last appearance in his home town, and his last in the Midlands for two and a half years. Promoter Ron Gray tried to stir up support for the promotion on the day of the fight when he realised that only half the tickets were sold, and he faced a £3,000 loss. The scheduled opponent Michel Stini pulled out again to be replaced by tough Frenchman Jacques Chinon. He had eight wins from twenty-nine fights including loses to former Sibson victims Sonny Kamunga and Gerard Nosley. Although Chinon had a less than impressive record up until then it is worthy of note that after this contest Chinon went fifteen fights undefeated, winning and retaining the French middleweight crown. Sibson was clubbed to the floor from looping lefts in the first when caught off balance and was performing in a subdued fashion until left hooks brought about bad cuts to both the Frenchman's eyes, forcing the referee to halt proceedings in the eighth. Sibson and Gunns both conceded that they'd under-estimated Chinon. Tony told Alan Parr of the Mercury "I was too casual at the end of the first and was hurt. I couldn't seem to get through him. He covered up well and it was only in the last round that I banged the uppercut through the middle. He was a much better fighter than his record suggests. It was a good fight for me because I learned a couple of things." Gunns added "Chinon was a very good opponent. He was tough and he could punch and Tony knows he must work on his defence. He was caught a couple of times and it might have been serious."

It was summer time and young Sibson having endured a torrid few months, and in the knowledge he'd have to defend his belt against Kevin Finnegan, sauntered off to Benidorm for eight weeks camping with friends. However, after a few weeks Tony called his mother who told him there were people trying to locate him to defend his title and advised him in no uncertain terms to get himself home. He had been pleased to get away from all the pressures, the training, the constant attention and discussions about forthcoming fights. Tony took his mother's advice and made his way home.

Sibson then had to knuckle down quickly to prepare for the defence against Finnegan on 9 October at the Royal Albert Hall. Ken Squires was becoming more involved in getting Tony fit and seemed to have the knack of being able to keep his nose to the grindstone. He now had Tony training in a small skittles alley at the rear of the Queen Victoria Hotel in Syston. However the day before the fight Finnegan pulled out with a back injury sustained while training in Copenhagen with world middle-weight contender, Ayub Kalule.

Carl Gunns summed up the feelings of the Sibson camp

when he told the Mercury "I feel very sorry for Tony. He had worked tremendously hard and has boxed eighty-three rounds with various sparring partners over the last two weeks. It's a terrible blow at this late stage and I have demanded a full enquiry from the Boxing Board. I also feel shattered for Tony's fans. They have spent a lot of money on tickets to see a title defence."

Mickey Duff and Mike Barrett brought in a late replacement to face the Leicester champion, a Puerto Rican called Willie Classen. On the surface Classen was a good opponent with sixteen wins from twenty-three fights. His only loss inside the distance was in his last fight six months previously. He'd went the distance with Eddie Mustapha Muhammed (then known as Eddie Gregory) and Vito Antuofermo, then world middle-weight champion. However he arrived in Britain without his licence, it being suspended by the New York commission due to that previous stoppage defeat, and a drug addiction. Two doctors brought in by the Board of Control passed him fit to fight and although no licence was available they allowed the fight to continue, based on the medical reports and his boxing record.

The fight was over in the second round after Sibson had knocked him over twice. Programmes were tossed into the ring by aggrieved spectators who'd paid hard earned cash to watch a competitive bout, and Classen was booed to the rafters of the old arena. The Puerto Rican complained of double-vision after the fight and was advised to attend Moorfields Eye Hospital but ordered the taxi-driver to take him to his hotel instead. When Classen and his manager returned to New York they told the

Commission that Sibson had won on a cut eye and managed to get another fight with top notcher Wilford Scypion on 23 November. He was stopped in the tenth of that one after a beating in the previous round and collapsed afterwards. At the hospital doctors discovered he had bleeding on the brain and never regained consciousness, dying five days later.

The match with Finnegan was put back to 6 November, and Ken Squires describes just what the problem was for Tony, or any other championship fighter, when this type of thing happens. "When you train a fighter for eight weeks for a big fight, two or three days after the fight, the fighters' gone and you've got to give him a break because you've built him up to a peak, and that's passed. He reached a peak for Willie Classen and if he'd fought Kevin Finnegan on that night, he'd have stopped Finnegan. You train a fighter up and a couple of days later, if you looked at them you wouldn't believe they're the same fighter. You've got to give them time off, not a long time, but then you've got to get them back in the gym. Then you've got to get them fit to actually train! Tony, he loved food you know. If you saw what he could eat you wouldn't believe it. Although he was training, he would sneak food. He was training, but he was eating and nobody knew about it except him. You couldn't look at Tony and see fat, he would put it on all over. He'd go missing and miss a day in the gym or something. You'd phone the house and he wouldn't be there. I'd find him, and pick him up in the morning drive eight miles away and leave him to run back to the gym. It's a little bit awkward being the trainer, and the manager is arranging things. You would never arrange a fight so soon after the previous one, especially in these circumstances. The promoters have a date to fill, and that's just the way it is."

The shambolic nature of Sibson's preparations for such an important first defence of his newly won Lonsdale Belt beggars belief! The day before the fight Ken Squires and another Belgrave worthy, Scottie Jordan, being suspicious of Tony's weight, put him on the gym scales and this revealed that he was eight pounds over the middleweight limit. These were old bathroom scales and they didn't trust them so they went down into the cellar of the Belgrave Social Club and found scales they used for weighing the beer barrels. Sibson remembered telling Ken "I'll be all right. I wasn't bothered. I hadn't been training. I wasn't even thinking about it. I'd had a bad experience in life and nothing mattered. We weighed in, and I was about three-quarters of a stone overweight! I was about twelve stones four pounds or something. Ken told me I wasn't going to make the weigh. I told him I'd had enough of boxing, that everybody was having my trousers down and that I could get by in life without boxing. Someone told me to say I'd hurt my leg and couldn't fight. Someone half-jokingly offered to whack me on the leg with a piece of wood to make my leg swell up for a couple of days. Just enough to fail a medical I smiled and thought "that's a bit extreme!" But I wasn't bothered. I said no. I had three-quarters of a stone to take off, and I said I'd have a go at taking it off. I went straight down to the chemists, got some laxatives and water tablets and then sat in my mate's health club sauna until it was time to leave Leicester about eight o'clock. I was dead. In London there were five of us in a double room – me, Carl Gunns, Ken Squires, Jim Knight and Les Anderson, the cut man. I'm sharing the bed with Ken and Carl, poor old Jim is in the chair and the other bloke is on the floor. I didn't get any sleep. I was starving and de-hydrated. Then when I did drop off, Ken woke me up. We had no scales to check my weight, so Ken took me out for a run just in case. I got just inside the gates at Hyde Park and I sat down on a bench and said I wasn't going any further. I felt dizzy and ill. Truly bad. I walked back to the hotel and I told Ken I didn't care anymore. We checked out of there before the weigh-in and I was eleven stones three pounds or something, way inside. We had a few photos and I was in a haze. I went to a place next door or somewhere and got a steak and kidney pie and some chips. But the drugs were still in my system and it went straight through me. We had to walk around until the fight time and we went to this museum. I felt weak as a kitten, I couldn't even get to the top of the steps. I just sat there, then found a bench and lay on it all afternoon. I tried to get some rest, but I knew I'd blown it. I thought about professional boxing, the whole show of it, and I thought I wouldn't treat a dog the way I'd been treated. I was just low, really down. I kept thinking about why I'd had that first fight for £85. The fun had gone out of it for me , by then. After the Lucas fight I packed in work as a brickie's labourer for Uncle Pete and Terry and tried to concentrate on boxing, but it never happened at that time. I was just playing at it, looking back. There was no one there to discipline me, no peers, as Jim Knight had retired and Ken was in full-time work, and I was running around with mates."

There is no escaping the fact that Tony himself had a lot to answer for in finding himself in this situation. While he might have been disillusioned by the whole business, and even though he may have felt he was letting a lot of people done if he'd announced he was walking away, he could and should have drawn out of the Finnegan fight weeks beforehand. He's right in thinking that he had older and wiser advisors nearby, but they can't shoulder all the responsibility. It is simply incredible to think that Tony went into a fifteen round British title fight in that condition.

The challenger, Kevin Finnegan was thirty-one years old and with two previous victories in British title fights was trying to win the Lonsdale Belt outright. He had been fighting for money since 1970 and had been in forty-three fights, winning thirty-three. In 1974 he'd won both the British and European championships, and claimed another British title victory three years later when he stopped Frank Lucas. Three months after this fight with Sibson he would regain his European crown. He was a formidable opponent for the young Sibson, even if he'd been fully fit!

It was a surprisingly close fight given the circumstances. It was exciting only in short bursts with the highly experienced challenger knowing just enough to edge a lot of the rounds. Tony was over reliant on his left hand and the wily old pro nullified a lot of these blows. Sibson didn't show any of the pre-fight weight draining concerns however and looked light on his feet responding fiercely every time Finnegan looked to be taking the initiative. At the end of the bout some of the media had Finnegan well in front although referee Harry Gibbs, scoring the contest himself, gave the fight to the older man by only one round. It was tough, gruelling sort of battle over fifteen rounds with both men earning their purse the hard way.

Unknown to the viewing public, and the boxing media,

Sibson was wondering all along if he'd manage to hear the final bell. "Kevin was trying to make a fight of it, but I was just happy going nice and smoothly through it. I didn't want any aggravation or trouble. I was just wanting to get through the fifteen rounds and not get filled in. When I knew I was near to the end I had a go. It nearly worked. I had him shell-shocked, but he wouldn't go. I couldn't sustain it. I had been drinking more than I was gargling."

Sibson became friends with Finnegan and gave his view on his general feelings at the time of the fight and how he felt much later. "Now, after all these years, I don't regret losing that one. Knowing Kevin as the man he was I'm glad he got a Lonsdale Belt outright. He's a man who deserved so much more out of boxing than he got. In my little way, it was a plan to end my era with Carl. Not planned as planned, but it was in my mind that this would have been a good thing if he won a Lonsdale Belt outright. Even the shape I was in I knew he couldn't hurt me. I should have kept my job labouring because that would have kept me fit. Really, at the back of my mind going into the Finnegan fight I was thinking if I lost it'd not be the end of the world because Finnegan would get the Lonsdale Belt he deserved and it'd give me an excuse to end my contract with Carl. Kevin was a good man, before the fight he was laughing and making light of things. In the ring after the fight I said to him, 'You'll need to show me some of these old tricks.' He thought I was wanting a re-match and he said he'd fight me again. I told him he'd got the wrong end of the stick and explained that I wanted him to show me things. I wanted to go where he had been without making the mistakes." As it turned out this brief exchange in the ring after fifteen tough rounds may well be the reason new avenues opened up for Sibson shortly thereafter, given Finnegan's London connections?

Sibson's short British title reign had come to an end and it seemed that this result would signal a change in direction in terms of Sibson's professional relationship with his manager Carl Gunns. Gunns had managed him from the very start of his career and now it looked like the end was in sight. No matter how the split is interpreted the fact remains that Carl Gunns took Tony Sibson to the British middleweight championship and when their contract ended Tony had become a major draw in British boxing.

A sourness had crept in, and on 29 November Tony turned up for a fight at Liverpool Stadium with Ken Squires, but no Carl Gunns. How far their relationship had deteriorated is emphasized in the following tale. "Carl told me the fight was for £1,500. I told him to say I wanted £2,000. And when I understood that had been agreed, I took it. When I got there, just me and Ken Squires, no Carl, I was sick. Charles Atkinson, the promoter, said it was £1,500. We eventually struck a deal at £1,750. He said to me, 'Think of the sport'. I said 'Stuff the sport. It's done nothing for me.' And I meant it. I felt so bitter then."

In the opposite corner to Sibson was American Robert Powell. He had eight fights, five wins and had never been stopped. Two minutes and fifty-four seconds after the first bell the sad Powell was lying crumpled on the canvas punished by body shots from an angry, frustrated, vicious, former champion.

The promoter said years later "Normally when a main event

ends in the first round, people boo and give you some stick. That night Sibson was so good they gave him a standing ovation. They raised the roof." Sibson recalled "There was just me and Ken and what I gave out were my true feelings. I just walked through him, went through him like a dose of salts. We stopped off in a chip shop and laughed all the way back to Leicester. It was like being kids again, being bank robbers or something. I paid Carl off out of that fight."

Out of this sad turn of events we can still find some humour over Tony's sweet tooth. A few weeks after the Finnegan debacle, Tony drove Mickey Bell, his brother Billy and their dad down to Milton Keynes where Mickey was due to fight Sylvester Mittee. After the show Billy and Tony chatted up a couple of waitresses and managed to persuade them to give up a jar of coffee and a twelve inch apple pie. They got home about one in the morning. The next day Mickey and Tony met up, and Mickey asked what had become of the pie. Tony replied that when he had got in he'd warmed up a full tin of custard, poured it over the pie and scoffed the lot! You couldn't write the script could you?

CHAPTER 6

All Roads Lead to London

The boxer/manager contract lasts for three years, with an option possible if the manager has secured a title victory for his fighter during that period. Carl Gunns, of course, had taken Sibson to the British championship, but their relationship had broken down and it was probably best for all concerned that there should have been a parting of the ways.

As 1980 approached people within boxing new that Sibson's contract with Gunns had ended and it's entirely possible that, following Tony's brief chat with Kevin Finnegan at the conclusion of their fight, word may have circulated around the London boxing gyms that Sibson was looking for a change of scenery. Tony believed that promoter Mike Barrett had shown an interest in becoming his manager and he knew that possibility was not for him. He voiced this opinion at the time "I'm not having that, it's not happening being tied to one promoter. No way I'm signing for a promoter whose going to use me when he wants me to fill the bill."

Mike Barrett persisted in phoning Sibson at home in an effort to secure his services but these offers were continually rejected. Then local Leicester boxing figure, Mick Greaves, who knew Tony and his family called round at his house one day. He told Sibson that London fight manager Sam Burns had been on the phone to him enquiring about Tony. Sibson had no idea who

Burns was, but Greaves explained he was Kevin Finnegan's manager and that he had also managed former world middleweight champion, Terry Downes. Tony was in a dilemma because he was really hoping that Liverpool manager Charlie Atkinson would come in for him.

Sibson thought there would be no harm in listening to what Burns had to say, and he was invited down to the Metropole Hotel near Lord's cricket ground one Sunday lunchtime. Tony drove to London himself with an idea of what he wanted to hear. He told Burns about the money being offered by Mike Barrett and Burns pointed out that this would tie him to the one promoter. Burns laid out his plans and Tony admits now that he was in *dreamland*. Burns told him he would be put up in a flat on his own. He would train in a gym at the Craven Arms in Lavender Hill with the very experienced coach, Freddie Hill, and fight regularly on the big London shows. Signing with Burns as his manager would mean that he would not be committed to any promoter in particular. The young, impressionable lad from Leicester saw the *bright lights* shining in front of his very eyes and knew then where he was going. The lights didn't even dim when his car broke down on the road home costing him £200 for repairs!

As well as signing up with Sam Burns Sibson took a huge step for a young man in those days by taking out a mortgage for £14,000 and bought himself a cottage in the village of Queniborough just to the north east of Leicester. Tony remembered his father's reaction well "I was out of a job, living on boxing revenues. My dad blew up and I don't blame him. I fell in love with the house, but I couldn't afford to live there.

Unfortunately the bloke I rented it to lost his job and couldn't pay the rent and it took ages to sort it all out. But I'm glad I did it now. It was a good investment to have."

With his boxing future now committed to London, he had to move south and occupied a flat suggested by Sam Burns. However Sibson didn't move into his own flat. Instead he was billeted with a lovely couple, Roy and Christine Clewer, who he grew to like and respect. Also in the flat were fellow boxers, Johnny Kennedy whom he knew from Derby, and Jackie Turner, a featherweight. Tony got on well with them all, but it wasn't what Burns had promised. Roy was a boxing fanatic who helped out at the gym Tony would use, with his wife running a ladies' keep fit class when the boxing sessions finished. "They were a lovely couple, wonderful people. I was so glad they were there. Roy was boxing mad, which drove me a bit crazy sometimes, he was keener on it than me. It can't have been easy for them, because as well as me they had John Kennedy and Jackie Turner from Hull. We were all young lads."

Tony trained at the boxing gym in Lavender Hill under the watchful eye of veteran coach Freddie Hill. Sibson's expectations were high. He had listened to the promises made by Sam Burns, he was now based in London and was quite literally a full time professional boxer. He thought he would learn so much more under this new regime and progress quickly. He quickly sensed however that things might not work out as he hoped.

His first difficulty was the loss of independence. He'd previously lived by himself in a flat in Leicester where he'd been self sufficient. Now he was sharing a room with two others and getting his washing done with meals prepared by Christine. Then the anticipated improvement in technique and ringcraft failed to materialise. With reference to Freddie Hill Tony said "Freddie Hill was a technical trainer. He concentrated on teaching techniques, which meant I wasn't working as hard, physically. I needed hard graft, a *full on* fitness regime. Freddie's methods never worked for me. Just about all he told me was 'stick your arse out.'" Sometimes boxers and new trainers simply can't gel together. Boxing history is littered with examples. Hill was a highly respected trainer and had over the years been involved with a string of world class fighters. It might be that he saw rough edges in Sibson's work and tried to correct them, but Tony had been taught everything he knew by Jim Knight, a man he held in the highest regard. Before leaving Leicester Sibson had begun to get used to training under Ken Squires and there is no doubt that he enjoyed a special relationship with him. Squires could motivate him to train to his limits, something no one else could manage up till then, nor indeed afterwards. While working out at the Craven Arms Tony felt he was not being pushed. It must be remembered that until fairly recently Tony had still been working on the building sites and felt this kept his strength up. With Hill spending time trying to improve his technique Sibson obviously thought something was lacking in terms of his fitness.

This was emphasized when Tony had his first fight under new management at the Royal Albert Hall on 22 January. His opponent was James Waire from Los Angeles. Waire was a tough opponent having won fourteen of nineteen fights and being stopped only once, in his second fight. Sibson weighed in at just under 11st 10lb and he recalled "I was a real porker. I lost four pounds in Freddie Hill's gym before that one." Sibson won over ten rounds, on points, dominating proceedings by using a deceptively clever jab against his much taller opponent.

The following evening Tony was on hand to receive the Boxing Writers *Young Boxer of the Year* award and would have been pleased to know the Boxing News now had him ranked number thirteen in their world ratings.

Notwithstanding the fact that the new arrangements were not entirely to Tony's satisfaction, his new manager did put together a title challenge in very quick order and the arrangements in Freddie Hill's gym must have been achieving something because, of course, fighting for a title meant he would have to make the middleweight limit. Sibson was matched with another Zambian Chisanda Mutti for the Commonwealth title at the Empire Pool, Wembley on 4 March. Mutti had an obscure record. According to official statistics, he'd only turned professional a year previously losing his first fight to Frank Lucas in Zambia. In the second of only two fights since, he'd secured the Zambian title, which apparently earned him the right to challenge for the Commonwealth version. Nobody really knew how many fights Mutti had, but he would go on to be a world class fighter at both light-heavyweight and cruiserweight, challenging twice for the IBF world cruiserweight crown. He would also lose eventually to legendary heavyweight champion Evander Holyfield.

Sibson prepared for the fight sparring Johnny Kennedy, Frankie Turner and a lad called Johnny Huntley whose parents owned the Sevenoaks Hotel. Huntley was very tall and used to spar with Kevin Finnegan. Tony remembers that Huntley even though he never fought competitively was a useful boxer who simply enjoyed working out in the gym. More importantly Sibson's sparring now included rounds with the new European champion and the man who took his British title, Kevin Finnegan. Finnegan of course was also trained by Freddie Hill and managed by Sam Burns.

Sibson remembers that Mutti was extremely tall for a middleweight and that both had to boil down to make the middleweight limit. Mutti, because he should have been fighting at light-heavyweight, and Sibson, because he was eating the wrong food and not working hard enough to lose the excess.

In the ring, Mutti, in his black shorts with white trim and towering over Sibson, looked every bit like an old experienced light-heavyweight from the 1950s. Despite looking dangerous with a crisp right hand counter whenever Sibson stepped back the Leicester man dominated the first half of the fight behind an impressive jab. Mutti made a comeback in the later rounds with long rights and uppercuts indeed he caught Sibson with a strong right hand in the thirteenth round causing a large swelling under his left eye. At the end Tony had secured the Commonwealth title by four clear rounds. Sibson suffered an unusual injury during the fight. "I stood on his foot in the second or third round and went over on my ankle but because of the adrenalin I didn't feel a thing. The following day I couldn't walk on it." Winning the Commonwealth belt didn't have the sense of achievement we might have expected for Sibson. "The title itself didn't mean much, they give Commonwealth championships away with raffle tickets! But it was a good feeling to be champion again. It meant I was getting back. I was going somewhere again."

Sibson's training was suspended for a couple of weeks following the Mutti fight with good reason. He was off to Las Vegas to support British hope Alan Minter in his quest to wrest the world middleweight crown from Italian/American Vito Antuofermo. Tony travelled with a real boxing crowd from London including Kevin Finnegan, Johnny Huntley and former world middleweight champion Terry Downes. As you would expect young Sibson had a high old time to himself visiting Caesars Palace and other casinos. After Minter's famous victory the new champ joined the *London mob* in the bar with his hard won belt.

During the fight Tony had been up on his feet cheering on his countryman to a great win but on his way home he must have realised how Minter's victory opened up so many possibilities. Although there would be the inevitable *return clause* for the new champion it was likely that Minter's promotional team could secure further defences in Britain. With Kevin Finnegan holding the British and European titles and Sibson wearing the Commonwealth crown it would have been easy to imagine the possible scenarios.

In the short time since Sibson had moved to London his travel itinerary had altered somewhat. While journeys in the car to Wolverhampton, West Bromich and Birmingham had been routine, it was now Las Vegas and Munich! Unfortunately for Tony neither of these trips had him on the promotions. The visit to Las Vegas was obviously to cheer on Minter, but the journey to Munich, with stable mate Kevin Finnegan, was for his

European title defence on 14 May against the German, George
Steinherr. Sibson remembered that visit well. "I loved Kevin
Finnegan. I could relate to him so fully. I used to go running
with him in Munich, but it was all over for him by then. We used
to run a hundred yards and he would say 'Shall we stop and do
a bit of shadow boxing?'. I'd say 'Come on, you've got to do
something', and we'd do a bit more. I was having to help him
through. We would run maybe half a mile in the morning, train
a bit in the afternoon, then sit in the sauna at night. We used to
share it with a handful of nude German models. We'd have some
fun, no hanky-panky, just a laugh. And I remember blushing
when Kevin told them I was a star of the future. I felt stupid
because it was his show. He was the star."

Despite the less than professional build up to the fight,
Finnegan still managed a draw and retained his title with the
Boxing News front page featuring a photograph with him being
hoisted on the shoulders of Sibson, who acted as a corner man
during the fight, with gym sparring partner Johnny Huntley.

The Boxing News headline – *Bernardi shows up flaws* –
following Tony's fight with Puerto Rican, Marciano Bernardi, is
a suggestion that perhaps the move to London was not all it was
cracked up to be. Reports were suggesting that Freddie Hill was
teaching Sibson how to *bob and weave* more, and coaching him
how to keep steady pressure on the opposition without relying
on the occasional bursts. Tony's experiences of that time were
remembered differently however. "I made them fights the
hardest fights ever. I was a seal in there, I don't know how I got
away with it. I had a bad eating condition, I did. I was a kid, and
when I went down to London I said 'Cor, let's have it!' I was

eating myself out of house and home, I was. I swear, Freddie Hill had a sauna through the back, and I used to sit with Kevin as regular as clockwork and Johnny Huntley sitting there sometimes for a bleeding hour on the day of a fight, not once but every, every time. We had a great laugh though, at the same time. My mate Wally Woodhams and Lenny McLean would be there doing impressions of Norman Wisdom and Tommy Cooper. It was a joke – I was a joke. I was being self destructive because it wasn't what I was looking for, I wasn't happy, it wasn't what I was looking for. I was paying for it now, I was damaging myself."

The fight with Bernardi took place at the Royal Albert Hall on 3 June. The visitor was a very useful opponent. From twenty-seven fights he had lost only five and drawn one with sixteen of his wins coming inside the distance. When Tony first saw him he was surprised at his height. "I couldn't get my bleeding arms round his waist!" Sibson won a difficult fight clearly but had to battle all the way. He ended up with cuts above and below the left eye and afterwards told Bob Mee "I had gone to the gym for the Bernardi fight and it should have been one way traffic but the training was doing nothing for me. For the first time I got black eyes, I got thick lips, I was cut too. He was a hardened campaigner but I should have eaten him alive. He was easy to hit. If it had been the days when I had just jumped off the scaffolding and laid into him I'd have beaten him easily. It's just that I wasn't working in the day and I was going to the gym at night and not doing enough. I thought after that 'Get out of it now, Tony' – but I didn't."

The summer break was looming large and Sibson knew he had to find something to fill his time. A good friend from the

gym, Brian Hill, got him a casual job on a building site before
he finally settled down for the summer back at his old trade,
hod carrying, with Bovis Construction. While happy working
and making new friends on the building sites his boxing
training was suffering because he simply wasn't turning up to
the gym in the evenings. Around this time Freddie Hill
phoned Sibson's parents in Leicester and told them Tony
wasn't training and that he was mixing with drug users in
Piccadilly. Sibson denied this emphatically. "I was not. I was
damn well working. I wasn't going to the gym, that's true
enough."

A few days later, and having no knowledge of Hill's
telephone call, the young *Jack the Lad* got a rude awakening
when he eventually visited his parents in Leicester having been
absent for some eight weeks. "I had a beard, but it didn't mean
anything. I walked into my man and dad's house and there was
this ghostly silence. My dad looked at my beard and said 'Get
that thing off.' I said 'It's only a joke, a laugh, dad'. I knew if
he'd have got up out of his chair he'd have punched my brains
in. My mam didn't even want to look at me. I went upstairs,
shaved it off, went to my mate's house and spent the whole
weekend getting drunk. I didn't know what I'd done wrong. I
was really hurt."

"When I got back to London I went to the gym and
everybody was laughing. They told me what had happened and
it was all a big joke. Freddie Hill was in San Remo with Kevin
Finnegan. And a good job too. If he'd been there I'd have wrung
his neck. I've been wild in my time, but I've always kept it out
of my mam's house."

Although probably a bit of a cliché, this was surely the straw which broke the camel's back, as far as Tony's relationship with Freddie Hill went. But before the end finally came, Sibson had another fight engagement to fulfil. He was scheduled to fight Irish American Ted Mann on the undercard of Alan Minter's world title defence against Marvin Hagler.

This gave Sibson had his first opportunity to watch Hagler at close quarters because the future star was offered training facilities at the Craven Arms gym. Tony along with others used to watch Hagler's workouts and they were all impressed with how hard he trained. He gave the impression he could go on training indefinitely. There were no opportunities for the local lads to spar with Hagler and as fight time approached he politely asked those using the gym if he could train and spar on his own. He had brought his own spar mate with him, Bobby *Boogaloo* Watts. Although hugely impressed with Hagler's workouts, Sibson looked on with some envy because he knew there had been times in his short boxing history when he'd been willing, and able, to accept all the physical training given to him back in Leicester. During the week leading up to the fight Sibson had an injury scare when he hurt his wrist while sparring with light-heavyweight Johnny Wall, but, after treatment from a Harley Street specialist, he was declared fit.

The night of 27 September at Wembley Arena has gone down in boxing folklore for all the wrong reasons. Minter was outclassed and brutally stopped on cut eyes in the third round but that was just the beginning of the drama! The late Boxing News editor Harry Mullan's report is probably the best description of what happened. "The long dead myth of British sportsmanship was finally buried at Wembley as a cascade of beer bottles and cans showered the ring and a racist mob howled obscenities at the black fighter who had taken Alan Minter's world middleweight title and at the black referee who had stopped the fight. For the first time in a British ring, and probably the first time anywhere, a new world champion had to be rushed from the ring as soon as the fight ended, without even waiting for the official announcement of his victory, to save him from actual physical attack by the crowd. There was not a shred of excuse for the behaviour of the lunatic fringe who bombarded the ring, or the larger element who behaved from the start as if they would have been more at home on a National Front rally. We had jingoistic nationalism of the worst kind. This was the ugly and unacceptable face of British sport."

Tony's fight took place earlier in the evening. Original opponent Mann had already been replaced by Peter Courtney before another substitute, Bobby Coolidge stepped into the breach. The American also had an impressive record. He was undefeated in eleven fights, winning nine inside the distance. Sibson laboured against the southpaw from Wisconsin, but in the seventh round knocked him over and the fight ended with a vicious left uppercut which left the stricken fighter flat on his back and unconscious. While it was an impressive finish the disgruntled Sibson said "I laboured against a no-hoper. I went out in the seventh and said 'Right, let's get this out of the way. Let's finish him.' But I didn't feel I was going anywhere and I wasn't giving the people who were coming down from Leicester the goods. I was fed up. I wasn't in my own backyard any more. I wasn't Tony Sibson any more. I didn't know what was happening." Alan Parr at the Leicester Mercury reported an astonishing outburst by Sam Burns after the fight. Parr, in Sibson's dressing room, heard the manager exclaim "Call yourself a fighter? If you carry on like that, you can pack your bags and go back to Leicester. It shouldn't need an old man like me to tell you what to do. It was a splendid finish but you messed about too much. This was your chance to shine and it's a good job you knocked him out. Your saving grace is that you can handle southpaws. So you'd better get yourself in shape because you're fighting for the European title next!" Was this Burns' back handed way of telling Tony he had secured a European title fight for him, or was he genuinely critical of his preparations and performance? Perhaps both!

The crunch time had come for Tony, and he'd made up his mind about going home to Leicester. He obviously had to confront Freddie Hill and as might be expected it didn't go well. "I went to the gym and said 'Look Fred. I'm going back to Leicester.' I knew I couldn't win if I stayed. I'd never been so unfit in my life. I told him nicely and he said 'Well, go on then, clear off, but don't expect me to take any raps for you.' He was insulted. I couldn't believe it. I stood back in amazement. He walked straight into the gym and slammed the door in my face. I didn't care, I thought 'That's it, it's done' and went home." And home as far as Sibson was concerned meant Ken Squires.

After Kevin Finnegan had lost his European crown to Matteo Salvemini there was an immediate agreement that the Italian's first defence would be against Tony Sibson at some later date. Sibson remembered his thoughts when he learned of the Salvemini fight. "There was no way I was going to win that fight.

I weren't even going to win an Area title ever again! I was a roly-poly."

Sibson buckled down to his training in a skittle alley at the rear of the Queen Victoria pub in Syston just outside Leicester. "It was an ice box," said Tony "no ring, no ropes, we just chalked a square out. I punched the bag and Ken invented circuits for me. The only sparring I had was with Ken's son, Kevin." Spartan though these conditions were Ken Squires had the *midas touch* as far as training Tony Sibson was concerned. Within a few weeks he was back to full fitness and raring to go.

A couple of weeks before the fight Sam Burns summoned Sibson to London so he could check his condition. "I went down there" Sibson recalled "and something I've never done before, I took charge, serious charge, of every sparring partner in there because I had worked hard and got myself in shape. I think I was 11st 7lb on that date and that was nearly two weeks before the fight. I went in there, I mean I didn't take liberties but I just wanted to show them I was wasting my time down there. I was back staying with Roy and Chris, well within five minutes I took my eye off the ball. I banged on half a stone in a matter of days. I just got back in the car and drove off back to Leicester. I said, tell Chris and Roy I'm off. Shadow boxing, punching the bags and sparring at night didn't do it for me, I needed physical exertion, it's the way I'm built."

So it was back to the skittle alley for Sibson under the watchful eye once again of his Leicester mentor. If anyone wants to create a mental picture of Ken Squires try to imagine the Burgess Meredith character in the early *Rocky* films, mixed with a vision of a typical Physical Training Instructor (which incidentally, he was!) from the days of National Service, and you'll begin to get the idea. There is a story that Ken returned from South Africa to Leicestershire in the 1950s and applied for a council house in a particular area. The application was refused so Ken pitched a makeshift tent in a nearby wood and lived there until the neighbours complained. The council tried to evict him but he refused to go until they had allocated him a house. He got the house!

Squires is as straight as they come, and to him a spade is a spade, not a shovel! Brought up in the same Belgrave area of Leicester he had a natural affinity with Sibson and expressed this opinion to Bob Mee. "I looked at Sibson and I saw power. Even at seventeen or eighteen the power in his body was there. If he hadn't gone pro so early he would have been ABA champion. I devised training routines for Sibson with Sibson in mind. When he chopped at a tree it was with an axe that had a fourteen pound head on it. I know my fighters. If Sibson had walked through the door and had a headache I'd know straight away. I don't fall in love with them and I like to bend them. If they are laid out in my gym, they aren't laid out in the ring!"

On the day before the Salvemini fight Sibson still had to sweat it out in a sauna even though he'd been put through his paces back at Syston. Tony dispelled any thoughts he wasn't ready. "I was fit though. It was just the last bit. Ken had worked me to death and I was fit enough to rule the world. Well, I thought I was."

The Salvemini contest was a great opportunity to really put Sibson on the world map. A win would install him as the European champion, and with the Commonwealth title already in the bag he could virtually be guaranteed meaningful, if not title fights, for the foreseeable future. Naturally his purse money would increase in proportion. However, a victory was not guaranteed. The Italian had won all his twenty-two fights, seventeen inside the schedule, and of course he'd dethroned Kevin Finnegan the last time in the ring. He'd fought three previous Sibson victims, stopping Jacques Chinon in seven rounds, stopped Jimmy Pickard in the same round and knocked out Al Clay in the second. Importantly, though, he had never fought outside Italy.

The fight on 8 December packed out the Royal Albert Hall and the fans were not disappointed with their night's entertainment. Unknown to anyone however, Tony had decided to experiment against Salvemini. He'd watched Hagler training at Lavender Hill and studied the way he moved in the ring. He thought he would try this out against the Italian and very quickly discovered that it wasn't working for him. This change of plan didn't upset the course of events thankfully. The fight proved to be an exceptional performance from Sibson with Salvemini being outclassed. The champion was down twice in the fourth round, with the Spanish referee inexplicably ignoring the timekeepers counting, allowing the fighter to continue when over ten seconds had elapsed. At two minutes and forty-eight seconds of the seventh round, after receiving a battering from a fired up Sibson, a right hand landed flush and the now deposed champion fell face first with no chance of beating any sort of count. Immediately afterwards Sibson told the Boxing News "I feel a new man, a brand new fighter. Before I was getting it all wrong, but now I know what fitness is all about. I'm not fat and ugly anymore!" At long last the trade paper acknowledged the progress and potential of Sibson with their front page banner headline reading, *Destroyer* over a photograph showing Tony launching another attack on the worried looking Italian.

There was a downside to the *coming of age* win, and the problem was one which had emerged before. In previous visits to London Sibson's large Midlands following had made themselves known. Up until now they were given the benefit of the doubt in most quarters as being simply vociferous and perhaps over exuberant supporters of their local hero. It may also have been the case that hardened boxing journalists and TV commentators recognised that Tony's followers were not used to attending big boxing tournaments and didn't quite understand the established etiquette for such occasions. This time however the reporting was different.

Once again the forthright Boxing News editor, Harry Mullan, did not *miss them and hit the wall.* In his report of the fight he said "The ring was instantly filled by a mob of his supporters who leapt and scrambled over the press benches, feet flailing. It was the same kind of ignorant, loutish behaviour we had from them when Sibson won the British title in this ring, and they bring little honour to their hero." Strong words indeed!

It had been a strange year for Tony. It started with the great anticipation of moving to the *bright lights* of London seeking fame and fortune, and ended just where he wanted to be with two titles, good money coming his way and an exciting future ahead. But in between he had the disappointing experience under the tutelage of Freddie Hill, the homesickness which

eventually drove him back to Leicester, and a growing
resentment for manager Sam Burns.

At this time Tony would have struggled to put into words his
overall feelings about how his boxing career was unfolding. He
had, and still has, a heart warming naivety which causes him to
expect people he views as friends, to be sincere in their dealings
with him. That's the way Tony himself would treat friends, in a
totally honest and straightforward way. Unfortunately the
naivety emerged when he expected associates in the boxing
world to behave in a similar manner. He simply couldn't accept
how those around him treated him and others as simple
commodities. He was and still is upset at Freddie Hill's reaction
when he told him he was returning to Leicester. He was similarly
disgusted with Sam Burns on a number of accounts; demanding
that he return to London a couple of weeks before the Salvemini
fight to *check* on him, implying that he didn't trust either him
or Ken Squires to prepare him properly; refusing to move out of
London occasionally to visit Tony at the gym in Leicester; and
putting Freddie Hill and Denis Pinchin in his corner for the
Salvemini fight, leaving Ken Squires outside the ring handing
up the *spit* bucket.

CHAPTER 7

A New Middleweight King is Born

Sibson was living in a rented flat in Leicester awaiting the rental agreement he had with tenants in his Queniborough cottage coming to an end, and training away happily with Ken Squires in the local skittles alley. Brother Troy would give Tony a lift into Syston and train himself in the background with Squires' son, Kevin, waiting until his more famous sibling was finished before taking him home. Ken Squires recalled that Troy himself wasn't a bad boxer himself and thought about getting him a professional licence at one point.

Reading reports in the boxing press was not something Tony was used to, but he must have been aware of a surprising letter which appeared in the Boxing News early in 1981. It is said that the worst thing a football manager can hear when his team is going through a bad spell is the club Chairman giving him his unreserved support. It usually means that his sacking is imminent! Freddie Hill trained Sam Burns' fighters, and Burns' reasons for writing a public letter to the Boxing News in support of his trainer are not clear. The letter carried the headline – *Trainer Hill Still Tops With Sibson*. In it Burns makes mention of "inaccurate statements which have been made by the media as a result of Tony Sibson returning to Leicester to live after a period in London." He goes on to state clearly that the reasons for Sibson returning to Leicester were due to him being unable to *settle* in London. Burns was clear in his support for Hill, "a person for whom I have the greatest respect and who has trained all my fighters since the early 1960s." He proceeded to also offer the support of Tony when he wrote "you can take it from me that Sibson has nothing but admiration for Freddie Hill and will be the first to admit that he improved considerably under the latter's instruction."

Once again Tony was off his mark early in the year with a fight at the Royal Albert Hall on 27 January against Argentinian Norberto Cabrera. This was a shrewd piece of matchmaking because in 1979 Cabrera had taken Marvin Hagler eight rounds before retiring. He'd also gone the full distance with Frank Lucas in a career which had seen him win twenty-four of his thirty-nine fights. Sibson won on points over ten rounds. It was a case of controlled aggression from Sibson and determination not to get stopped by Cabrera, but the fight started with a shock for the European champion when he was bowled over without taking a count in the first round from a right hand counter. The fight was won convincingly, but afterwards Tony was critical of his performance. "Everything went so well in the gym. I think the shock of actually having a height and reach advantage over an opponent threw me off. I felt such a berk being put over in the first. The punch actually hit me on the neck and I was caught off balance. I was never hurt during the whole fight and if nothing else, I learnt a hell of a lot tonight." Some days later when he had time to reflect he commented on his opponent "He was tough. I just boxed him out of it. I tried to do him in eight rounds like Hagler had, but I couldn't. It was supposed to be a step up in class, but it didn't feel like it. He was a good campaigner, but nothing special."

In the middle of February the Boxing News published their unofficial world ratings which found Tony ranked number eight with Minter, Dwight Davison, Hamsho, Antuofermo, Obelmejias, Parker and Fletcher all lining up behind Marvin Hagler in the middleweight division. It is also worth observing that ranked number three in the world at light-heavyweight was Lottie Mwale! Tony was now also tied into a European title defence away from home in Spain against the mandatory challenger Andoni Amana on 1 May. London promoter Harry Levene lost the purse bids with the Spanish promoter presenting Sibson with a £16,000 pay day (valued at £50,000 in 2012).

It was not a comfortable relationship between Sam Burns and Tony. It's clear that the experienced London fight figure saw himself more as a manager in the traditional business sense than an employee and representative of his boxer. His role should have been that of a modern day football player's agent. Tony explained how their relationship caused friction. "I was under a lot of pressure to stay in London, I'll tell you! I was told straight 'what do you think you're about?' I was Freddie Hill's bread and butter. He wanted me there because he wanted his 10%. I said to Sam Burns 'I'm training like a lunatic with Ken and he wants to take time off work to work on some things' and Sam said 'Oh no he ain't, because you're coming back up here. We want to cast our eye over you to make sure everything's all right.' I told Sam 'Every time I come down there I'm half a stone over weight.' I told Sam I didn't want to do it, no disrespect to anyone but it wasn't the dream I thought it was going to be. The gym, all the lads, they were great, Lenny McLean used to come down, Billy Walker, I had a great time. I used to go out with Kevin Finnegan and Wally Woodhams and we had a great time. I once stayed at his house for about a week but nobody knew what I needed. I needed somebody to keep my nose to the grindstone because I needed motivation."

It is easy to understand now where each party was coming from. Tony wanted to be back home in Leicester because he knew that Ken Squires was the one man who could get him to the level of fitness he needed to perform at his best. Sam Burns knew that he had a *star* in his stable, one who if managed properly could earn everyone involved a lot of money. He didn't know Ken Squires well, and there was a danger, in his eyes, that Sibson might not be getting the coaching he needed. Freddie Hill was an extremely experienced and respected boxing trainer who had guided several fighters to world class level. He obviously suspected that Sibson had a tendency to go off the rails and thought that he could handle him best. All through boxing history there have been famous partnerships between particular champions and their trainers; Ali and Angelo Dundee; Yank Durham and Joe Frazier; Rocky Marciano and Charley Goldman; Terry Lawless and Frank Bruno; Manny Pacquiao and Freddie Roach etc etc. Sometimes a fighter just seems to respond to a certain type of person and for Tony that person was Ken Squires.

Tony was less than impressive in his next fight on the undercard of Alan Minter's comeback at Wembley Arena on 17 March. The original opponent was to have been Nick Ortiz but due to a problem with his flight tickets a substitute in the shape of Andre Mongelema from Zaire was drafted in. He had eight wins and four draws from his twelve fights, but had taken former Sibson victim Jacques Chinon to a draw only two months previously. Although he would lose six out of his next eight fights after Sibson, he would go on to win the French middle-weight title, beat Matteo Salvemini, and lose a challenge for the European title after twelve close rounds in 1989. The Boxing News reported that Sibson looked *fleshy* a sure sign that things were not going well behind the scenes. Nevertheless he was good enough to win six and draw three of the ten rounds, and there were the occasional bursts of hooking to keep the crowd reasonably happy. In the meantime Minter's long road back to world title contention had begun with a sold win over world rated Ernie Singletary.

Although not an inspiring performance from Sibson he did earn his highest purse to date, £6,000 (around £18,000 in 2012) so Sam Burns was holding his end of the bargain up by getting Tony regular fights with good money.

Sibson's next outing was the risky European title defence on 14 May in Bilbao against the number five ranked contender Andoni Amana. The Spaniard was moving up from the light-middleweight division where surprisingly he was still listed as the number five in the world by the World Boxing Council. There were added difficulties for Tony, or any other British boxer, travelling to Spain for a fight. In fact the Board of Control were refusing to allow *anyone* to fight there unless it was for a title. Over the previous three years a series of British fighters had travelled to Spain and been treated disgracefully including incidents which almost led to promoter Mickey Duff being

arrested for protesting, and an elderly Board official being
kicked in the groin by security staff. Tony though, against the
wishes of his advisors, insisted on the fight being put out to
purse bids which were won by the Spaniards. Tony recalled that
Sam Burns' was apprehensive. "Sam said to me 'Don't be stupid.
You go across there and you'll lose the title.' I said 'I'd sooner
have a few quid. You leave the rest to me, Sam.'"

Amana had been in forty-four fights, winning forty-two but
had never fought outside Spain. There were two common foes,
Jacques Chinon whom Amana had stopped in five rounds and
Pat Thomas, with the Spaniard again winning that one, this
time on points.

Sibson had prepared well under Ken Squires for the fight but
by the time the party reached Spain the same old problems
emerged. "Making the weight always kills me, but this was a
nightmare. I left Leicester at 11st 9lb. I was thinking about
losing a pound and a half and then drying out overnight, but
when we got there I got on the scales that Sam had and I was
12st 2lb. I went mad. I knew they weren't right, but nobody
would have it. I was starving myself and Sam was on about
dehydrating me and getting me a sweat suit on, giving me
nothing to eat. I was screaming and yelling and Sam did a u-turn
and walked out of the room. I had a row with Ken and told them
both 'Get out of my life, just get out.' I'm not a nutter, but I
cracked then. I took the phone out of the wall, tipped the room
out completely and slung the scales out of the window. They
landed on the roof of a garage. I stayed in that room for a day
and a half and they just left me alone. Then I went for a walk. I
just needed to get my head sorted out. I was light headed and I

was gone all day. I went into the centre of Bilbao and calmed myself down. I had a sandwich and a cup of coffee. I fed the pigeons. Then when I was ready I went back. It turned out that they had sent a search party out for me. I can't believe it all happened now. We got some different scales and the weight was right."

Present day boxing fans would find these circumstances, and those before the Kevin Finnegan fight, incredible. Nowadays top level boxers have full time nutritionists in their camp where not only their weight but their body fat content is measured daily. The regulating bodies now check the fighters weights at regular intervals leading up to the fight date to ensure their weight is reducing within safe limits. Also, and perhaps controversially, the official weigh-in is held twenty-four hours before the fight thus allowing the boxers time to rehydrate if necessary.

What was equally incredible, but perhaps more laughable, were the conditions meeting Tony and his team when they were ushered into the venue, a bullring, for the fight. Tony can remember them well. "I'm in this stable, I swear to God, there are piles of bullshit from the day before. I couldn't believe it. I thought, what's going on. It hadn't been cleaned out for a week or two. I'm sitting there, and I said 'Somebody's taking the piss.' Somebody said 'No this is the changing rooms.' In the end I looked at Ken and we just laughed. 'I'm not staying in here.' I went into the passageway to warm up. I took a chair out into the passage way. 'I'm not sitting in there.' Talk about my amateur days, I never had anything like this, bullshit everywhere. But Ken kept me focussed, all the pad work and the rest of it. We got into the ring and the noise was unbelievable, all those Basques."

The twenty-three years old Sibson was becoming a victim of his own success. He was after all the current European and Commonwealth champion, and former British champion, but an awful lot was expected of him every time he stepped into the ring. This title defence turned out to be no exception. After flooring Amana in the second and again in the seventh Tony won a clear unanimous verdict from the three foreign judges but still the Boxing News correspondent considered that he had an "off-night" and "made hard work of it." Even Sibson joined in his own criticism by adding "It was the first time I've boxed abroad, and I was very nervous. The crowd made so much noise that I found it hard to concentrate properly. I never really got into my rhythm, and I'm sorry for the crowd that they didn't see me at my best. I can fight ten times better than I did tonight."

It also appeared that someone else may have been a bit over critical as Sibson explains. "When the fight finished Sam Burns said 'We've lost that.' I said 'You what?' He said 'We've lost that. You're not on home territory now.' I said 'I've beat him, I've boxed his head off.' He said 'No, you've a bad cut, you've lost.' Sibson obviously couldn't believe what his manager had said and was mightily relieved when the result was announced. Tony remembered the exact circumstances well. "We're in the middle of the ring, the ref's put my hand up and the other kid's dropped to his knees. He's got his hands up as if pleading to the crowd to forgive him. I thought 'Christ what chance have I got of getting out of here alive!'"

Trainer Ken Squires had fond memories of the Bilbao trip. When referring to the fight Ken recalled "Amana thought he were going out and he was glad he got to that bell. The fans thought Tony was fantastic. Do you know them heels they have? It wasn't clapping because it was thunder. All these heels stamping all the way round this bullring. It was marvellous." Ken also disassociated himself from the general apathy about Sibson's performance saying "Double hooks, a good right hand, good rolling, backing him up. The bloke didn't really want to get involved too much. He did a good job."

Most boxing people in Britain still considered former world champion, Alan Minter, to be the top middleweight in the country. And why not? After all he had been fighting at world level for a few years and was being guided to a rematch with Marvin Hagler. He'd beaten top ten rated Ernie Singletary, and in Las Vegas on 6 June he was due to fight Mustapha Hamsho, with the winner promised a match against Hagler. However it did not turn out the way the Minter camp had hoped. Minter lost on a split decision over ten rounds. Two judges gave the fight to Hamsho by seven rounds to three, while a third scored it for the Briton by six rounds to four. This meant that later in the year Hamsho, and not Minter, would be challenging for the world title. Sibson may not have fully realised the implications this result would have had for him.

During the summer of 1981 the big fight under discussion for British fight fans was undoubtedly a match-up between Minter and Sibson. Frank Butler, guest writing for the Boxing News, claimed that promoters were bidding £100,000 for the fight (roughly £300,000 in 2012) which would be guaranteed to sell out any arena in the country. The following week Minter had this to say about negotiations "I'm the name, I'm the one

that can sell out Wembley. Why all the talk of a 60-40 cut for
Tony? Look what I've achieved, who I've fought. If Tony wins
he's up at the top, if he loses he can still come again. The fight's
a step down for me. I gave up the European title for bigger
things."

The fight was announced on 31 July, as being fixed for
15 September at Wembley Arena. Only the European title
would be at stake and already the *war of words* had started.
Sibson commented "This is my chance to come out of the
shadows. I'm hungry for success and I'm taking this fight
because I don't want to go back to a nine to five job. I've got a
lot of respect for Minter but I think he may have slipped a bit.
The old spark didn't seem to be there against Mustapha
Hamsho." Meanwhile Minter had his own views. "I couldn't
retire without facing Sibson. People would say I deliberately
ducked him. I've sparred with Sibson. He's strong but I think I
hit harder. I also think his boxing had gone-off since he moved
back to Leicester."

It was ominous that Minter should mention retirement in his
comments about the fight. Why would he even think about it if
that wasn't already on his mind. He'd had a tremendous career
starting with the winning of a bronze medal in the 1972
Olympic games. Minter suffered horribly with cut eye defeats
all through his career but won the British title in 1975 and
successfully defended it three times securing a Lonsdale Belt. He
then twice won the European title, losing it once through a cut
eye, before going on to beat Antuofermo for the world title. He
beat Antuofermo again before eventually losing it to Hagler.

Ken Squires had his own views about Minter. "I don't know

about Alan Minter. He was a big, static boxer type of thing. If you look at the England amateur set-up at that time they were all dead correct and, all right, they were good, but he still had that sort of style for me. I worked on Tony for that fight and there were one special move. I had Tony move that lead foot, roll out and pivot up, not over the top but pivoting upwards with a hook. It worked beautiful on Minter."

There seems to have been little wrong in Sibson's build up to this fight. "I was that fit. Apart from the Hagler fight, I was equally as fit. Without question the energy was bouncing off me. Anyone whose had that feeling will know what I'm talking about. All those cheating ways I had about me were gone. I used to do a ten mile run, dry out, meet my mate Wayne Elton down the swimming baths, do about two miles swimming. He used to set circuits up, using your legs then using your arms, breast stroke, front crawl with a weight between my legs. I couldn't believe you could come out of the water sweating, pumping out of me. I was amazed. Then I'd go home, walk the dog, come back have a kip get ready and go down the gym with Ken. We didn't do a lot of sparring, just on the bags, the pads maybe, a bit of sparring at the end with Tony McKenzie."

Although the fitness preparations were going well Sibson's old mental demons were still lurking. He remembered going down to London on his own for a pre-planned press conference with Minter and the event did not go according to the script. "I was on my own, all my mates were working. I got to the place, went round the corner and there's Alan with his Rolls Royce, his wife with him, his bowler hat on, he looked like the man, a big star. I don't possess that, I didn't know how to do that. He obviously loved it, it's part of the ingredients he needed for success. Anyway, I went round the corner and I looked and thought 'There's no way I'm going in there, I'm off!'. I phoned a mate Wally Woodhams who I had met when I was training at Lavender Hill. I told him I didn't fancy the press conference and I'd come down to see him. We had a right night out. Went to see Johnny Binden. We all went out together and had a great night. We went to a place called the Gasworks in Fulham till the early hours of the morning. I got the train the next day, got back home, took me a day to recover from that and then I went back down the gym with Ken."

Of course there would be no avoiding the press conference and another was arranged. "I got a bollocking from Sam Burns for not attending that one, so I went down again to show respect to Alan. Alan, he fancied it. His wife was there keeping us apart. He was trying to come again don't worry about that, but you know what, I sort of found the ingredients." There were other distractions too in the build up. Well known boxing figure Dennie Mancini contacted Ken Squires and asked if Tony would do a photo shoot for Lonsdale Sports, the famous boxing retailer based at Beak Street in London. Down he went and modelled their equipment, and later both Ken and Tony were grateful when proprietor Bernard Hart sent up a whole shipment of training items for use at the gym in Syston.

Wembley Arena was packed for the fight with both boxers earning a reputed £80,000 (£240,000 in 2012) each. This was a massive event for British boxing and crucial for Sibson. Minter had been fighting at world class level for several years, while Tony was virtually unknown outwith Europe. A Sibson victory would launch him into that status and raise his profile significantly. For once, other than his fight in Spain, Sibson's loyal fans were outnumbered and the old champion favoured in many quarters to still have enough left to see off the young pretender.

The fight started as most people expected with both boxers feeling each other out and being sensible enough not to take too many chances early on. Tony can remember clearly the fanatical shouts of encouragement coming from his pal at ringside, Kevin Finnegan, but not much else. At the end of the round Sibson came back to his corner and Ken Squires remembered what Tony said to him "Lovely, seen it." What Sibson was telling his corner man was that he had seen the opening for the move they had been practising to deliver, the punch Ken Squires had nicknamed, the *pivot hook*. The punch which was actually a hook-cum-uppercut.

The Boxing News report suggested that the turning point in the fight came at the midpoint of the second round when Ken Squires' *pivot hook* landed with a jolt. Sibson fired several bursts of hooks after this and took the round. The brief conversations between Squires and Sibson continued in the corner. Tony told Squires "Seen it, done it, and now I'm going out here to work!" Sibson explained that going out for the third round he felt *superhuman* and knew after landing with *the punch* in the last round that he was going to win.

Sibson stormed out of his corner at the start of the third and soon had Minter backing off. After about a minute Sibson pinned Minter on the ropes and unleashed a series of right and left hooks, before a vicious left hook caught the Crawley man flush on the nose and down he went. Minter bravely got to his feet, winked at his corner to show them he was all right and prepared to fight back. It was to no avail because there was no stopping the Leicester man. Sibson did not let up and fired volleys of hooks all of which were now landing cleanly. The last salvo caught Minter and down he went again, this time in serious trouble. The referee seeing his distress dispensed with the count and waved the fight over at one minute and fifty-nine seconds.

Sibson celebrated his victory, but once Minter had recovered, he went over to the new star and congratulated him. Tony put into words what his thoughts were at that time. "I respected Alan Minter. I went over to see him fight Antuofermo and was rooting for him, screaming for him to win. He said to me some nice, good things after the fight, he said, 'Don't let me down get them done'. I said 'We'll see how it goes.'"

Minter picked up the ring microphone and spoke to his large following. "I would just like to say I'm sorry it didn't last too long, but the punch he caught me with was a blinder. I think that punch would have knocked out anyone in the world tonight." Minter never fought again!

It can be surprising what boxers remember about the aftermath of certain big fights and Tony's recollections are no different. "I'm in my changing rooms and Harry Carpenter is trying to do an interview with me when all of a sudden the door bursts open and it's Freddie Starr. He pretends he's Muhammad Ali and he's screaming 'You've got my title, you've got my title', and all the while he's shadow boxing. Well that's it, the interview's over, isn't it? I couldn't believe it. Harry Carpenter says well we'll get back to business. I told him 'I'm done mate.' He weren't a fan of mine anyway. With Freddie Starr it was hilarious, I'm crumpled on the couch and in tears of laughter. I did find out he was a big Alan Minter fan and he went back to Alan's and spoke to Alan and no doubt made him laugh as well. I just wanted out of the bleeding place after that. The adrenalin makes me feel sick so I'd sooner get out so that I'd calm down."

Sadly the fight, although televised by the BBC, was never shown. Minter's camp had worked out a deal with DAF Trucks for their name to be displayed on his shorts. The BBC would have none of it. Minter's people tried to put sticking plaster over the logo but it kept peeling off during the fight and at the end of the day the BBC refused to screen the fight due to their stance on advertising. It's somewhat ironic that their decision caused so much of a stink in the national press that DAF probably got more publicity than they had anticipated.

While a studio guest on a television programme in 2012, Tony listened while Alan Minter told viewers how he woke up in bed with the pain in his nose on the night after the fight. When he got up and looked in the mirror he knew something was seriously wrong because his nose had swollen grotesquely. He had to attend hospital where they diagnosed an aneurism. When the camera turned to Sibson it was obvious he'd never heard the story before and was absolutely horrified that he'd caused a fellow professional so much distress.

Interest was now beginning to mount on a potential challenge by Sibson to world middleweight champion Marvin Hagler. This was demonstrated with the decision by Odeon cinemas to show his 3 October world title defence against

Mustapha Hamsho live on their screens, not only in Leicester Square and East Ham in London, but funnily enough in Leicester! Tony visited the Leicester Odeon with friends and saw Hagler stop the brave Hamsho in the eleventh round. A couple of weeks later the Boxing News had elevated Sibson to the position of number two contender for Hagler's crown, one place below Hamsho.

Tony had worked out that it might be more profitable for him if future European title defences were put out to purse bids in the hope that, following his profitable trip to Spain earlier in the year, another foreign bidder could come in. There was confusion with this process but regardless of these issues the next defence against Italian Nicola Cirelli was destined for Wembley Arena on 24 November.

Cirelli was viewed by many before the fight as a *routine* challenger for Sibson. In his twenty-five fights, he had won them all except one, crucially a technical knockout loss to Salvemini for the Italian title. There were two other common opponents, Jacques Chinon whom Cirelli stopped in the fifth round and Sonny Kamunga, whom he beat on points. Sibson was suffering from a back injury in the lead up to this fight. "I couldn't lean back, Ken tried to take me on the pads and my breath would stop. I couldn't believe it. When I leaned back I thought my lungs had been cut off. I thought 'I'm going to have to pull out of this fight,' but you couldn't, could you? You've a fight and that's it. I got plenty of massage but I missed a lot of training and I wasn't sharp."

Before the fight Ken Squires had been studying Cirelli and reckoned he wasn't robust, even a bit soft looking. The trainer's

instructions to Tony were to go out and capture the centre of the
ring and dominate the fight. In fact, to make his point, when
they got into the ring before the fight, Squires walked to the
centre and stamped his foot down on the canvas, leaving a
temporary indentation on the canvas to emphasize to Sibson
where he wanted him to be. As it turned out Cirelli was a top
drawer opponent who used his long reach to repeatedly catch
Sibson with jabs and quick left hook whenever he tried to move
inside. Cirelli was certainly not *soft* as Squires had imagined and
took some stiff shots from Sibson without folding. Although
winning the rounds Sibson was not dominating and the half-
filled Arena saw a relatively close contest. That was until the end
of the ninth round. As the bell approached Sibson threw a long
right hand which thumped into the head of the Italian. As he
staggered backwards Sibson launched a left hook which landed
right on the point of the challengers chin, sending him to the
canvas with a clatter. Tony's momentum took him down as well
and he had to jump to his feet quickly. The Italian bravely
struggled up to beat the count and just as the bell rang his corner
appeared to throw in the towel. The referee ignored this gesture
of surrender and both boxers came out for the tenth. Almost
immediately Sibson went on the offensive catching Cirelli
cleanly with a succession of hooks and a final vicious blow ended
the fight.

The press acknowledged the quality of the finish but were
unkindly critical of Sibson's performance, perhaps due to the
challenger boxing out of his skin. Cirelli made a valiant attempt
to win the title and showed little regard for Sibson's punching
power.

Tony won the prestigious Boxer of the Year accolade from the Boxing News and deservedly so. He had five fights, three for the European title and won them all convincingly. He was now a star attraction in the big London arenas and rated very highly in the world rankings. Although there had been the acrimonious split with Freddie Hill and growing concerns with the money he thought he should have been attracting it was nevertheless an outstanding year in the ring. The pressure was growing for a world title tilt against Hagler, or if either of the two world boxing organisations were to strip him of his crown, then the 'movers and shakers' in British boxing were hopeful of including Sibson in any discussions about who should challenge for the vacant belts.

CHAPTER 8

Number One Contender

When 1982 came around, Sibson, now European and Commonwealth champion, had been fighting for five years and eight months and had taken part in an incredible forty-eight fights, seven of them with a title at stake. In comparison with two modern day champions, Ricky Hatton and Joe Calzaghe, over the same time span, the former had sixteen less fights and only one comparable title challenge, with the latter having twenty-one less fights and an identical number of title contests. Sibson had been worked hard even by standards of the time. His manager Sam Burns and promoters Duff and Barrett were determined there would be no let up as they tried to manoeuvre him towards world title contention as quick as they could.

That opportunity arose early in the year when they managed to secure a final eliminator for the World Boxing Council version of the championship. A joint promotion with American Carl King was arranged for the National Exhibition Centre near Birmingham on Sunday 21 February. The unusual day and time of the fight was to accommodate American television. In the opposite corner would be Dwight Davison from Detroit. Davison was a top level opponent with thirty-one wins and only one defeat. He'd beaten world class fighters in the forms of Willie Monroe, Curtis Parker and Wilford Scypion.

Mickey Duff said that if the Midlands fans supported the

venture he would move *heaven and earth* to get Hagler to defend his crown there in the event of a Sibson victory.

Tony prepared well for the fight and was able to watch videos of Davison's fights with Parker and Scypion. This might not have been such a good idea because Tony said "I saw his fights with Curtis Parker, Wilford Scypion and somebody else and he smashed them to pieces. They were all my shape and size, I couldn't believe it! I thought oh no, my God! I'd never watched fighters before in my life, what am I watching this for? I wish to God I'd never seen them. He absolutely murdered them. His arms were so long!"

Once again though Tony went *walkabout* for a few days during the build. Ken Squires felt that this was due to pressure from the media. "A lot of people were pestering him everbody's getting on to Tony. Ringing his phone, trying to get into the gym, even trying to photograph him in a wheelbarrow. He wouldn't have it, so he does a runner for a couple of days."

In fact Tony was off with his old Belgrave mates Mickey Bell and his brother Billy to visit the Bell's extended family in Dumfries where by all accounts they had a high old time to themselves. All three ate and drank to excess, but they knew that they'd have to go back down south sooner or later and when they did Sibson was in a far better place mentally. They also had an extra passenger, Mickey and Billy's grandmother, because she was going to support Tony at the NEC!

Squires prides himself in having an empathy with his fighters and told this story about himself to demonstrate the point. "We went to a press conference and there's a meal on afterwards. So we sit down and Tony knows he can't eat. He tells me 'You're not fighting you can have a meal.' I said 'If my fighters not having a meal, I'm not having a meal.'"

Tony remembered his meeting with Davison at the weigh-in. "He was a big guy, quite quiet, not pleasant, he didn't really want to know anybody. Then Don King's son, Carl, motor mouth, is giving it all the chat in the world. I never listen to that nonsense so it never bothered me. I got on the scales and Carl King says 'Too light to fight, too thin to win!' and I said 'Yeah, I'm here for the journey.'"

This was Sibson's first fight in the Midlands for two and a half years and he was welcomed back with open arms as 11,500 fans turned up to cheer him on. As Tony approached the ring his enthusiastic trainer Ken Squires was jogging along in front looking as if he himself was going to be fighting. As they entered the ring the huge arena erupted and at that point Davison, dressed all in green, must have felt very lonely indeed. As soon as the bout got underway Sibson charged forward throwing accurate jabs and left hooks, and for four rounds the visitor resembled someone ambling along a shopping centre casually gazing into the windows. He was slow, weak and seemed totally disinterested. When Tony landed with a hard shot Davison would simply grin and shrug his shoulders. What could have been the matter? His team did arrive late in England and missed the first pre-arranged press conference. Was he jet-lagged? Before the fight started Harry Carpenter could see a bruising under his left eye which was not there when he had arrived in this country, so he obviously sustained it in sparring. Was he weight weakened? Was there contractual problems with his management team, or did he underestimate Sibson? Did the large crowd intimidate him? We simply do not know but he was not performing like the world's number one contender for Hagler's crown.

Davison seemed to wake up in the fifth, sixth and seventh rounds landing big right hands on occasion and did try to force Sibson on to his back foot. Thereafter he sunk back into a daydream looking lethargic and wrapping his big long arms round Sibson when he could. At the end of the ninth round Ken Squires told Sibson "Listen you've not knocked this guy down and you've not upset him. So what I want you to do now I want you to go right back to boxing, sharp jabbing, sharp one twos, double everything up, I want everything back on speed and forget about knocking the bloke out, you're not going to knock this guy out."

The fight followed a similar pattern until the final round. It looked as if someone had at last mentioned to Davison that he was in a final eliminator because he came out throwing punches from every angle and threw caution to the wind. But it was far too late and at the end Sibson got the verdict from all three judges, in fact one judge deemed that Davison hadn't won a round!

It would be fair to say that Davison did not live up to Sibson's pre-fight expectations of him. "I thought he was going to come out, stamp his authority, and I would bob and weave and just try to smash my way through to him. I thought this is the only chance I've got, he's too long for me. Nothing's happening, I couldn't believe it. I'm hitting him with jabs, body shots, I'm even getting frustrated, disappointed because this is not the fight I've prepared for. It was doing my head in. I didn't like it at all, I thought bleeding hell something's going to happen. But I was sharp, on my toes, I could see them all at the ringside, Maurice Hope, Alan Minter, Jim Watt all those guys at ringside, it was a big event. But he just wasn't producing the goods. I wanted a *tear up*, I wanted it. I'd seen the video and I thought 'Let's have it!' He tried to do it in the last couple of rounds. A very disappointing fight for me because I had prepared so much for it."

It was however not all good news for the Sibson camp as boxing politics began to raise its ugly head. Mickey Duff told the waiting media that he would do everything in his power to bring Marvin Hagler to the NEC for a world title challenge by Sibson. New promoter, Frank Warren, who was struggling to break on to the scene said he'd also be bidding to bring the fight to the UK. Informed opinion suggested that anyone wishing to secure the contest would have to bid in the region of £1,250,000 (£3,775,000 in 2012). However Hagler, who watched the fight on American television, saw his national anthem booed and the chaotic scenes on the ring apron before the official announcement was made reminded him of the disgraceful circumstances when he took the title from Minter. Hagler told American journalists that he would not fight in Britain again.

On 7 March Hagler went through another challenger when he stopped William *Caveman* Lee in sixty-seven seconds. This was the fourth defence of his title since beating Minter and he was fast becoming not only the top middleweight in the world, but reckoned by many to be the best boxer on the planet. A huge fight in Canada against Tommy Hearns had being arranged for early in the summer which meant that any negotiations for a quick challenge by Sibson would stall. In fact that fight never took place and indeed was delayed for a further three years.

With Tony now settled in his cottage at Queniborough he was beginning to look to the future and considering ways to make his money work for him. He decided to go into partnership with his brother in law Alan Moore, a builder. They created a company, *Michael James Limited*, a combination of both their middle names, thus avoiding the use of the well known Sibson appendage. They found plots of land in attractive areas of the Leicestershire countryside and began to build houses, and with both having backgrounds in the building trade, got involved with the work themselves.

The problem for Sam Burns now was how to keep Tony motivated. He didn't want to risk his number one contender status, but at the same time realised that if Sibson was not focussed with a big fight looming he could quite easily go off the rails. On this occasion the problem was taken out of his hands because the European Boxing Union insisted on Sibson making another defence of his European title. His opponent for the 4 May was none other than former victim Jacques Chinon. Chinon was in the opposite corner the last time he fought in Leicester three years previously. Sibson stopped him with body shots on that occasion and in the build up to the return contest the Boxing News were particularly scathing in his right to challenge for the continental belt. This was grossly unfair on the tough Frenchman. Since losing to Sibson, he'd won twelve, drawn three and lost only once. That defeat was three months previously on points in Denmark to world class Ayub Kalule. Moreover he'd won and then defended the French title on five occasions. Hardly a soft touch!

It was another big night at the Wembley Arena and Sibson came out looking fit enough but lacking a bit of his usual aggression. In the second round Chinon opened up and Tony seemed to step back and look at the Frenchman thinking "you shouldn't be doing this it's not in the script!" There was a respite in the action when Sibson's boot laces became completely undone with the referee stopping the action to tie them again. In the third Chinon appeared to be growing in confidence and landed with several wild left hooks and these seemed to draw some anger from the champion. They stood toe to toe in mid-ring and Tony was lucky when massive left hook from Chinon missed its target. Sibson was performing like a car engine with dirt in the fuel pipe. Occasionally the blockage would clear and he would begin to fire on all cylinders but then a piece of dirt would lodge in it again and it was back to coughing and spluttering! Chinon landed with a solid right in the fifth which seemed to shake Sibson and encourage the challenger but the fight turned in the seventh when a vicious left hook by Sibson landed behind Chinon's right elbow. The Frenchman was clearly hurt and backed off followed by Sibson. The champion caught him with the exact same punch and Chinon was lucky to stay on his feet. It took Chinon a couple of rounds to recover but towards the end of the ninth and beginning of the tenth he was lashing Tony's ribs with long left hooks until a big left hook landed flush on his forehead causing him to stumble drunkenly back towards the ropes. Sibson began teeing off on Chinon and the referee interrupted to administer a *standing* count. Not long after it re-commenced the referee, perhaps a little prematurely, stopped the contest with Sibson successfully retaining his title.

It was only after the fight that his fans discovered that Tony had been nursing an injury to his right hand since the Davison fight. When he started training for the Chinon fight he could feel the injury and there were discussions about calling the fight off. However Tony knew that providing he landed the punch in a certain way the pain could be minimised. During the third round of the fight he hurt it again when he caught Chinon's elbow and he felt this unsettled him. The hand was so badly swollen that he couldn't have it x-rayed for a fortnight afterwards and his arm and hand were put in a precautionary plaster cast.

Notwithstanding the hand injury Tony himself was self critical of his performance, as he had been several times in the past. When he failed to produce his best form it hurt and embarrassed him far more than it needed to have done. He knew that hundreds of his loyal supporters, primarily from Leicester, but from all over the Midlands had spent good money in buying tickets and travelling down to London to see him fight. When he couldn't get the punches off to finish the fights in impressive fashion he thought he'd let them down and it would eat away at him for days and weeks afterwards. But, away from the ring, there were other de-motivating issues constantly on his mind.

For most of the last five years Tony was of the firm belief that he was being exploited. He could see the huge following he attracted to his fights and felt the income they were generating was filling other people's pockets. The issue is not whether he was being exploited or not, but the fact he thought he was, and that was enough. Boxing promotion is a business, that's the case as much today as it was then, and only a fool enters a commercial enterprise to lose money. Promoters expect to make a profit after all the expenses are paid. Likewise managers have certain functions to perform on behalf of their boxer and deserve remuneration, in fact their percentage from the fighters' purse is set at 25% by the Boxing Board. Similarly the trainer works hard to get his man ready for a fight and they too should receive 10% of the same purse.

These feelings hung over Sibson's head like a dark cloud. While other boxers in a similar situation can put those matters to the back of their minds, on many occasions Tony simply couldn't. He would lie awake at night and it would gnaw away at him. When he was in these moods, there would be two possible outcomes. Firstly he found that he couldn't motivate himself to train as hard or as regularly as he should have, and secondly he would 'comfort eat', neither of which is a healthy course of action for a championship boxer.

Tony was not the only one unhappy at the way they were being treated. Ken Squires remembered a conversation he had with Sam Burns over the heavy punch bag he had in his gym at Syston. When Tony had a session on the bag the whole gym shook and the other boxers training at the time would stop and watch. Of course the inevitable happened. After another night of pounding from Sibson's left hooks, the bag burst (these professional bags are usually around £250 to buy at 2012 prices). Squires phoned Sam Burns the following day asking for a contribution towards a replacement. Ken said that Burns' response was "Ken, you want to be a trainer, you've got to have the equipment to train, buy yourself a bag!" Now, it is debatable about who is responsibility for replacing the bag, but Ken

Squires is an ordinary working man training boxers every night
at his gym in an old skittles alley behind a pub, one of whom is
the European champion. Sam Burns was a wealthy elder
statesman of British boxing who had been involved in the
boxing business for years and seemed to live a very affluent
lifestyle based on his earnings. It would surely have been a
gesture of goodwill if he had offered something towards it. This
was a very minor incident but it serves to demonstrate the
relationships which existed. It would seem plausible to suggest
that Burns' had never fully accepted Sibson's move away from
London and perhaps believed that Squires was behind it?

The performance in the Chinon fight was a perfect example
of the effects this had. While being able to get down to the
weight limit and fit to go ten hard rounds, he nevertheless took
punches which he should normally have been able to avoid with
ease, and he was on occasion a fraction of a second slow in
getting his own punches away. The result was an easy fight,
made difficult, by his disturbed preparation.

Meanwhile the world middleweight title had moved into a
period of stagnation. Hagler's proposed fight with Tommy
Hearns in Ontario was pushed back to July before being
eventually cancelled indefinitely apparently due to Hearns
refusing to fight in Canada and Hagler refusing to fight in
Hearns' home city of Detroit. Further problems for Hagler
emerged when another defence against Fulgencio Obelmejias
was aborted after sparring partner Bobby Watts broke his ribs.
Back in Britain there was talk of Sibson being matched with
former Hagler victim Mustapha Hamsho and matchmaker
Mickey Duff was also in negotiations to bring North American

light-heavyweight champion, exiled Scot, Murray Sutherland over to London to fight Tony for his long dormant Commonwealth crown. At the end of July when the Sutherland fight fell through Sibson reluctantly gave up that particular title.

Ken Squires was able to explain what it was like with regard to upcoming contests for Tony at the time. "A lot of these fights, Sam Burns phones up and says 'He's in action on such-a-such date' and you don't know who he's fighting because if he gave you one name, then three or four days before the fight, he would say sorry, so-and-so has pulled out and they just chuck somebody else in. So when you get up to that level, where Tony is as European champion, if somebody pulls out they just phone around and they can get somebody overnight actually. But it didn't matter, I always had him fit for whatever date we had."

Finally Sibson's next fight was arranged for 14 September at the Empire Pool Wembley on the undercard of a Colin Jones European title fight. Tony's opponent was an unremarkable Chilean called Antonio Garrido. He had twenty-four fights, with five defeats and a draw, his only *claim to fame* being a recent victory over former, but faded, world champion Hugo Corro. It was not an inspiring match-up, but it did keep Sibson competing, and earning, prior to the potential fight with Hagler.

It was a disappointing night for spectators at Wembley. Colin Jones's European defence was cancelled and a poor Commonwealth contest was fixed up at late notice. In Sibson's fight with Garrido, for the first time, the Leicester man heard the sounds of a disgruntled crowd as the boos and catcalls began to rain down in the sixth, as he laboured to deal effectively with the constantly retreating Chilean, who was offering little resistance. The South American bobbed and weaved making Sibson miss wildly. After more jeering in the seventh, Tony came out in the next round and pummelled Garrido to the head and body. It was little surprise therefore when his corner pulled him out at the end of the round.

With the Commonwealth crown already relinquished, Sam Burns then contacted Tony and told him he was also giving up the European belt. Tony was *livid* believing that they could comfortably have squeezed in another defence before any proposed Hagler fight. Ken Squires called the European title Sibson's *bank account* and thought it would be foolish to give it away. Squires had studied the possible challengers on the continent and believed there was nobody in contention who could cause Tony serious problems. Burns meanwhile justified his decision by claiming he didn't want Tony to get beaten on a cut eye, or acquire some other sort of injury which would curtail the challenge for the world crown.

Negotiations for the Hagler fight were well underway and Tony insisted on having a say. Sam Burns was keen on the fight going ahead in England, possibly at the NEC, but in this scenario Sibson's cut of the purse would be greatly reduced. Tony therefore insisted that the bout be put out to *purse offers* meaning that the highest bidder would win the right to stage the fight. This turned out to be a wise move. The *winner* was American promoter Bob Arum who bid $2,100,000(nearly £3.5 in 2012) against a rival bid from Mickey Duff ($600,000, £1 million in 2012) and this resulted in Tony's split coming to £300,000 (£830,000 in 2012). Thereafter however, Arum tried to delay the fight, and offered Sibson three fights in the States on the undercard of Hagler defences at £60,000 (£160,000) each. Tony was up for this arrangement and recalled "I was offered $100,000 to fight anyone in the top ten, anyone of my choice. It was to be two or three fights on the undercards of Hagler bills, which would have brought me the experience of the atmosphere and showmanship of it all, and prepared me better for the big one."

Once ITV, which had begun to show boxing again, realised that a fight with Hagler was being arranged, they got their top commentator, Reg Gutteridge, to contact Tony and invite him out to San Remo in Italy, where Hagler was making his next defence against Fulgencio Obelmejias on 31 October. Sibson had a great time with Gutteridge who he said "made a joke out of everything" and was a "great old character." Hagler battered Obelmejias to defeat in five rounds and the following day Tony and Reg had a pre-arranged meeting and interview with Hagler at his hotel. Tony found Hagler to be *relaxed* and *friendly* and they spoke about the fight the night before. However, once the cameras were switched on and the *formal* interview started at the poolside of the hotel Hagler tried his hardest to be modest, and failed miserably. He came across as patronising and made it clear that it would be very unlikely that he'd ever fight again in London following the events after the Minter fight.

Sibson had one other matter to sort out. With the fight looking like being fixed for February, Tony was in discussion with his Leicester accountant, John Francis, about how to invest his purse. As a result, Francis wrote to Jarvis Astaire pointing out that Tony's purse would be taxed at 60% if the fight went ahead in the current tax year. There were suggestions about how to get around this issue including temporarily moving out the country or starting certain types of pension schemes, none of which appealed to Sibson. There appeared to be no way round this issue and by late November everyone knew the fight was on for 11 February in America.

Almost seven years after setting out on a professional career, *just for a laugh*, to give his friends an excuse for a good night out, Tony Sibson had secured the biggest pay day of his boxing career, and the chance to win the ultimate prize. Following a good, but not outstanding, amateur career, no one, least of all Tony himself, could have imagined where it would take him. While still only twenty-four years old, he'd engaged in a staggering fifty-one fights, won and lost the Lonsdale belt, won and retained the European title, won the Commonwealth title and soundly beaten the number one contender for the world crown. He'd earned his opportunity.

It is doubtful if anyone at the time, other than those closest to him, could have envisaged the effect the build up would have on the painfully shy Sibson. Training and sparring had never been a problem as long as he was motivated. In fact Tony often repeated his feelings on this. "Put me in the gym, just with Ken and a few sparring partners, nobody watching, and I could go all day." It was all the other necessities in relation to promoting the fight which worried Sibson.

At the end of the year the Boxing News carried four separate adverts inviting fans to travel to America to see the fight. Boston Promotions of Leicester were offering a £239 deal (£664 for 2012), Ace Travel had an eight days package excluding tickets for £449 (£1,250), Trade Promotion Travel in London had a four day package excluding tickets for around the same figure, and Fieldborough Travel in Loughborough had a one night package for £230 (£640). It seemed that there would be a large contingent travelling to America in support of the extremely popular British boxer.

CHAPTER 9

Marvin Hagler

Very few of us ever reach the pinnacle of our chosen career path. If it was easy then we would all be *captains of industry*, senior government officials, consultant surgeons, or Nobel prize winners and such like. Towards the end of 1982 Tony Sibson was one step away from that pinnacle and he knew how difficult a task it had been to get there and was determined to be fully prepared to meet the challenge.

Trainer Ken Squires planned his usual systematic training regime to get Sibson ready. Squires believed that there had to be two stages to the process. Firstly he had to get Tony fit enough to actually undertake the programme he had planned for him and then would come the real *boxing* training for the fight. So, in the build up to Christmas, he had Sibson running from his home in Barkby to woods outside the neighbouring village of Syston, where he had secured permission from the landowner to chop up fallen tree trunks. Squires arrived with the axe and Tony would set about the trees for three minutes with a minutes rest in between. A makeshift form of circuit training was added for good measure. Squires insisted that these types of exercises were needed for Sibson. "This was all about building up Tony's strength for his gym work to follow." Quite possibly Squires understood that Tony had been at his strongest early in his career when he'd been working on building sites during the day before training in the evenings. Squires' planning was so meticulous that he even considered the weight of the axe Tony would be using!

The *real* training commenced just after the New Year celebrations ended. The gym in Syston had undergone a makeover. The old skittles alley was converted thanks to help from Tony Everard, a senior official with a local brewery. He donated the materials necessary and with the help of local tradesmen they created a well appointed boxing gym. It was not *state-of-the-art* by any means but it suited Ken Squires, Tony and the other boxers.

The first few weeks were spent getting Tony back into his usual boxing routine whilst improving his timing. Hours were spent on the heavy bag (which incidentally had Hagler's photo plastered on to it), the floor to ceiling ball for speed and hanging speedball for co-ordination. As fight time approached, Squires brought in two of his light-welterweights for sparring, Tony McKenzie and Tony Richards, as well as a southpaw from Bedford, Mickey Kidd. The sparring partners would only box every other round, resting in between, meaning Sibson was always facing a fresh opponent. Also brought in to spar was Commonwealth games gold medallist, Chris Pyatt, who had just turned professional.

The detailed planning almost went up in smoke shortly before the party were due to leave for the States. Sam Burns arrived at the gym with a large press contingent from London with a view to publicising the fight. Tony turned up a bit later than expected which obviously upset Burns due to the time constraints with the press corps having to meet deadlines.

Squires remarked "Tony wasn't ready. He had just put his gear on when Sam Burns told him to get into the ring with this other lad. They met in the middle of the ring and the lad threw a big punch which burst Tony's nose. I shouldn't have allowed it but Sam made such a fuss because we were late. That was the last Tony sparred before the Hagler fight." Tony remembered the same incident. "I got changed straight away and started to spar. No warm-ups, nothing. I walked straight on to an uppercut from Cliff Gilpin. It was an accident. He wasn't looking to take any scalps. But he bruised my sinuses and enflamed my eyes. That was that. I got changed and walked out of the gym again. It was all over in ten minutes. I was really annoyed and I never sparred a day after that."

In the early 1980s, video recorders were becoming a much sought after household item, but they were by no means commonplace. To get a video recording of a boxers' fights was much more difficult than it is today, and although it would have been possible for the Sibson camp to lay their hands on one of Hagler, there seems to have been no attempt to do so. Modern British fighters travelling to the USA to fight for a world title will spend hours examining every aspect of their prospective opponents abilities, dissecting each punch they throw and how they defend themselves. But we should not be so surprised that this didn't happen. Tony says that there was very little emphasis on studying Hagler and added "I saw him often enough on the telly, and had been at ringside in San Remo."

Several weeks before the fight Ken and Tony set off by train from Leicester to London, meeting up with Sam Burns and cutman, Dennis Pinchin, a publican from Victoria Park near

Bethnal Green, who Tony knew from his days at Lavender Hill. The group then carried on to Gatwick for their flight to Boston. On their arrival they were picked up in a large limousine and driven directly to the Marriot Hotel in Worcester, forty-four miles away. The camp were allocated a well fitted out gym within the indoor sports stadium where the fight would take place. Ken Squires remembered "It was freezing with snow and ice and Tony would have to do his roadwork running round the corridor behind the terracing inside this stadium. I used to go out in front of Tony and he'd have to run after me and keep going till he caught up. A bit like a greyhound chasing a hare." However Sibson can also recall going down to the hotel gym one day and meeting a local marathon runner. They got talking and this chap knew who Sibson was, and offered to take him running round areas he used when he was training. The British fighter thoroughly enjoyed this, so much so that on one occasion they went too far and when they returned Ken Squires "gave him into trouble." Presumably the trainer didn't want him burned out before the gym work had even started!

In the lead up to the fight Sibson clearly recalls that he was very fit, had no complaints, and was raring to go. "There was some things in the background I wasn't happy about, but I was feeling great. I'd never been fitter. I knew Hagler was a top fighter but I was young and fearless. I had been winning European and Commonwealth fights when I wasn't even out of second gear because I used to let myself go between fights. I don't mean I was drinking but I used to eat like a pig. Sometimes I was up at thirteen stones. For this fight I was ready. I thought I would win it but I knew no matter how I did it, it would be really tough."

In the evenings the public and media were allowed into his training sessions. The American boxing press were disappointed that they didn't get to see Sibson sparring, a conscious decision by his camp. Tony admits that he felt uncomfortable with onlookers when he was training. He became self conscious and didn't think he impressed when sparring particularly with upwards of two hundred spectators watching his every move. Throughout his career he believed that sparring was a learning experience and only on a few occasions did he feel the need to punch with some force merely as a *warning shot* to someone *trying it on*. Because he wasn't prepared to lash into sparring partners he had the impression that outsiders might be critical of him.

About a week before the fight Tony got an unexpected lift when he realised one of his musical heroes, Johnny Cash, was performing a series of concerts at the fight venue. The camp's chauffeur, Michael, on hearing this, used his contacts and got Tony a private meeting in Cash's dressing room before one of his shows. Cash played a few songs for the awestruck Sibson who had to pinch himself to make sure he wasn't dreaming!

The homesickness began to get wiped away on the Tuesday night before the fight when 350 British fans, including former world champion Terry Downes, and Tony's mother and father, who were celebrating their silver wedding, travelled in eighteen inches of snow from Boston to watch an arranged training session.

When boxing people get together and discuss the best middleweights who ever lived, Marvin Hagler is in the mix. Although Hagler lost a disputed decision in his last contest to

Sugar Ray Leonard, and was refused a rematch, he nevertheless is up there with the greats of the division. The rough, tough Harry Greb was a middleweight icon from the 1920s, but modern historians have difficulty judging his greatness due to no film footage of his fights being available. Sugar Ray Robinson, who won and lost the middleweight title three times in the 1950s, is thought by many to be not only the best middleweight, but the best boxer ever. Nevertheless, it is unlikely that anyone involved in boxing would dispute that Hagler was one of the top five middleweights of all time.

Hagler was right handed but fought from a southpaw stance meaning that he jabbed and hooked with his strong, leading, right hand. When he got opponents in trouble he switched stance and threw the right with venom. In this respect he was much like Sibson. Tony was left handed, but like Hagler, led with his strong side. The man from Brockton, home of former legendary heavyweight champion, Rocky Marciano, and guided by Italian-Americans, Pat and Goody Petronelli, was a throw-back to the glory days of professional boxing in the States. He trained hard, brought the fight to his opponents and generally shunned publicity. There was nothing *flashy* about him. In other words he lived the life of a professional athlete.

In those days of fifteen round championship fights, Hagler seemed able to last the distance with room to spare, such was his fitness level. He was surprisingly light on his feet, punched very accurately, had inch perfect timing and a superb boxing brain which allowed him to control his fights with ease. His right jab could spring out, land flush, and be back in position before his opponent could react. As his fights wore on he would begin to put more *meat* on his punches, setting up those on the receiving end for the inevitable finish.

Shortly before the Sibson fight, Hagler had his name changed officially to *Marvelous Marvin Hagler* and when he produced the necessary paperwork, rumours emerged that he was actually twenty-eight years old, two years younger than previously thought. His new appendage was not a misnomer. He was indeed every inch *marvelous* and his forty-nine former opponents wouldn't argue.

This then was the man Tony Sibson would face for the world title in Hagler's own backyard of Massachusetts, USA. Hagler had won the title three years previously by destroying our own Alan Minter in London and made five successful defences since, all inside the distance victories. This was part of a thirty fight unbeaten run, going back seven years, with twenty-six of these wins coming by stoppage. Hagler was not a *one punch* concussive hitter but he nevertheless hit hard and often, with top level fighters being unable to withstand their cumulative effect.

As the night of the fight approached all 11,000 tickets for the Centrum Arena in Worcester had been sold, including some several dozen to Sibson supporters, including close family relatives. An appeal had raised funds for Tony's old trainer, Jim Knight, to travel. As expected Tony's most unusual fan, Swede Klaus Zell made the trip with his publican pal Barry Garrigan. A group from Luton, led by Olympic runner David Bedford, made their way up to East Midlands airport to join the throng. Back home in Leicester many hundreds made their way late, in the snow, to venues in the city including the De Montford Hall to watch the live satellite feed.

Ken Squires continues to be upset about the events immediately preceding the fight. "When you warm a fighter up in the dressing room before a fight and you're getting him ready for that fight, you're getting all the adrenalin flowing, and you're saying to Tony 'Come on Tony, we're here to win tonight,' we're talking to him, and working on moves. He's warm, you've got the adrenalin running, and then we're chased out the dressing room along these corridors into a big auditorium, down and into the ring. I gets him into the ring and he's looking good. Then we're waiting, and waiting, and there's no Marvin Hagler. He doesn't show. I turned round to Sam Burns and said 'What's going off here?' Because I've got the fighter ready, I've warmed him up ready for the fight but he's allowed now to go cold. I'm saying 'We can't stand about here in the ring, Sam.' We're stood there in the ring with the British flag and Hagler's not even showing! So in the end I'm saying 'Get him out the ring.' Now Tony's losing his concentration. He's saying 'Oh there's Uncle Pete, Jack Nicholson,' he's looking around the crowd. You don't do that, you get in the ring, you're warm, you're listening to your trainers, have a drink, those type of things and in the end the sheen's gone off him, he's cooled right down. I looked at Sam Burns and he looked lost, I couldn't believe it."

As both boxers shuffled around in their respective corners Sibson, despite the delay, looked serious and determined. There was strong support for the British boxer, well beyond the three hundred who had flown out for the fight. When the bell rang Hagler moved out in his southpaw stance and bounced to his left and right showing he was very light on his feet for a middleweight. Over the first half of the round Hagler landed three clean and strong jabs as well as an uppercut with a single left hook from Tony in reply. After a minor clash Sibson raised his glove to his head and indicated to the referee to be mindful of Hagler's head on the inside. At this stage Hagler was moving comfortably around the outside of the ring with Sibson stalking him. In the latter stages Hagler landed twice more with two solid jabs while Sibson responded with a left uppercut and a flurry with a single left and right landing. It was a close round but it must have been awarded to the champion on the basis of him landing the cleaner punches.

Sibson looked eager for the second round to begin and was instructed by the referee to get back to his corner to await the bell. Hagler got off the mark quickly and landed two solid jabs. The American seemed to be planting his feet more and Sibson took advantage launching three left hooks in succession, with only one landing cleanly. Sibson was trying to land his jabs but they were out of range. Hagler sprang into attack and led with a solid right uppercut followed by a long right hand, both of which landed solidly. Hagler was showing his adaptability as he moved into counter-attacking mode catching Sibson with right and lefts when his attacks fell short. The round reached its conclusion with a solid jab and a left and right landing on Sibson's head. BBC commentator Harry Carpenter thought this was a better round for the Leicester man but it's difficult to agree with his assessment. Hagler seemed to have outscored Tony convincingly.

In the corner between rounds Sibson took several gulps of water from Ken Squires and manager Sam Burns was pushed away by the trainer when he tried to replace the gumshield too early. Sibson was on his feet eager to get started, but the confident look had disappeared, and the first signs of swelling to his left eye appeared. However he was first to land with a nice left jab as the round followed a similar pattern with Hagler back on his toes and Sibson following after him. In this round Sibson began to find his range and landed cleanly with a left jab, a left uppercut on the inside, and a left hook counter. For the first time in the fight, Hagler went to the body and landed with a long right hook behind Sibson's guard. Strangely Hagler's jabs were falling short. The challenger went on the offensive landing with a left hook to the body and Hagler seemed to be backing off, although he did land with two right hands before the bell. The best round for Sibson so far, and he possibly just edged the session.

As Sibson came out for the fourth he appeared to glance down to his right and nod his head to someone sitting near ringside. The round started with both boxers circling and jabbing with all attempts falling short. Hagler did eventually land with a solid straight right and this provoked Sibson into an extended attack with nothing of note landing cleanly. Unusually for such an accurate puncher, Hagler threw a long right hand and missed wildly. In mid round Hagler scored with a solid, short right hook coming out of clinch and a few seconds later Sibson connected with one of his own. There was much more clinching in this round and Sibson appeared to have settled into the fight. With nothing to separate the boxers, this round could easily have been scored a draw.

At the end of the fourth, cut man Denis Pinchin, moved into the corner to join Ken Squires due to damage around Tony's left eye. The referee's attention was drawn by Sibson's corner to Hagler's protector which appeared to have moved up, and he had a word with the Petronelli's. Hagler came out as if he meant business and landed a vicious right uppercut followed by a powerful straight right. Hagler followed this up with a stinging left coming out of the neutral corner. The partisan home crowd began to sense a change in the fight as Hagler landed another solid right jab followed immediately by a right uppercut. Sibson attempted to halt the storm by swinging a right and left with both missing the mark, but it was clear that Hagler was stepping up the pace. Hagler scored with a short left and Sibson replied with one of his own. Hagler then threw three long raking right jabs in quick succession, bringing the crowd to their feet, and causing a cut around Sibson's left eye. It seemed that the challenger knew he was cut because he launched himself at Hagler landing four left and right hooks while in close. Both fighters were going for each other as the bell sounded. Sibson appeared to land just after the bell and Hagler glared at him. Tony patted both Hagler's cheeks in apology.

Due to Sibson's cut eye the doctor entered the corner to inspect it, but he did not seem too concerned. As he prepared for the bell, Sibson looked down at his feet and glanced again towards the ringside seats. He then banged his gloves together as if trying to psyche himself up. Hagler looked focussed and after missing with a wild left he followed with a right which landed with full force on Sibson. Another two right jabs landed cleanly but the brave challenger kept jumping into attacks, without troubling Hagler. Hagler was now refusing to give ground allowing Sibson to score with a right to the body and two lefts to the head. Nevertheless Sibson's cut was getting worse but he stuck to the task and landed another right and left combination before Hagler fired back with a right. The champion could see the damage and landed a long right on the affected eye. One minute and forty-nine seconds into the round the spectators saw the start of Sibson's demise. Tony bent forward from the waist to avoid Hagler but got caught with a thudding right hook to the side of the head and fell backwards on to the seat of his shorts. He was on his feet quickly and was walking across the ring as the referee tolled the compulsory *eight count*. Hagler, sensing victory, moved in but Sibson met him without retreating and scored with two solid left hooks on the inside. Both boxers met in the centre of the ring and let go with everything they had, and a right from Hagler caused Sibson's legs to buckle. As he bent over another wicked right hook crashed into the side of his head and he dropped to the canvas. This time he took a bit longer to get to his feet and when he did his back was facing the champion. Sibson was unsteady on his feet and when the referee looked into his eyes he immediately waved the fight over. A disconsolate Sibson wandered back to his corner as the ring was invaded by Hagler's fans.

In the immediate aftermath of the fight arrangements were made to have Tony's cuts repaired. The team drove behind a snow plough to the designated hospital where a top surgeon stitched the eye damage, inside and out. The following day there were murmurings of discord in the Sibson camp about preparations beforehand. Tony told Harry Mullan of the Boxing News "Everything went wrong. My cup split, and then I got cut so badly that I couldn't see the punches coming. I wasn't especially hurt when I was knocked down, but I was confused and he caught me square on. I feel so disappointed. I really believed I was going to be world champion, but I got well beaten. I felt as strong as a water buffalo, and I was in my best condition, ever, but it just wasn't there. Maybe it was a mistake not to spar. I never believed that anyone could do to me what Hagler did last night. I looked at myself in the mirror, at the cuts, the lumps, and the black eye, and I thought I never knew what fighters looked like before! He just knocked me all over the place. His punches were so accurate, and he made my mistakes look worse than anyone else could have done."

In addition to the sparring issue, or lack of it, Tony had another problem to contend with. The new protector he wore had apparently been re-stitched to make it a better fit and the stitches burst in the second round before finally coming apart at the first knockdown in the sixth. Sibson recalled "When I was knocked down it did finally come apart. I knew then I was in trouble. Sam Burns tried to make a great play of this at the press conference but I pulled the protector off him and threw it on the floor and told him to say no more about it."

Tony's friend from Leicester, Johnny Strong, tells a hilarious story about British ingenuity in the immediate aftermath of the fight. Strong was with a number of Leicester bookmakers along with the snooker player, Willie Thorne and was standing outside a hotel hoping to get into Marvin Hagler's celebratory party. Security at the entrance were checking guests and ensuring they had a stamp on their hand allowing admission. While standing there in the snow a limousine drew up and out stepped the former middleweight champion, Vito Antuofermo.

Using surprising enterprise, Strong stepped forward, removed Antuofermo's coat, shook the snow off it, folded it over his arm and ushered the boxer to the entrance. The doormen asked Strong how many were in the party, and on looking round saw around eight faces he recognised. They were all allowed in. Once inside Strong and one of the bookmakers known as Dangles were asked to go into the small room. They soon realised that this was where the bodyguards hung up their guns! Once inside the main room, they mingled with film stars like Lee Majors, and using the influence of Antuofermo, who now knew what was going on, managed to get inside the security bubble around Sugar Ray Leonard to get their photos taken, thereby winning a $1,000 bet for Dangles! You couldn't make it up, could you?

The morning after the fight manager Sam Burns re-arranged his flight home, caught a taxi to the airport and departed in such a hurry that he left behind his cashmere coat. Ken Squires had to wear it on his flight home because if he'd put it in with the luggage it would have exceeded the weight limit. Tony also left separately, this time with Ken's son Kevin, for a well earned holiday in Florida.

On reflection years later Squires mused "I feel, as I know Tony Sibson, having been in all those fights with Tony Sibson, I look at that fight and think, that wasn't Tony Sibson! Knowing what happened up to the first bell it took all the shine off him. He wasn't buzzing. He wasn't doing all that fast rolling, he was a different fighter. I mean I work the pads with Tony, I know him well. I've never seen anyone hit him with three straight jabs. We got turned over with the long wait. He would have been better to have taken the three fights in America beforehand. I'm definitely sure it would have been a war, I'm a 100% Tony Sibson could have beaten Marvin Hagler! We'd seen Marvin Hagler, he was good, but if everything had gone right, I'm sure he would have given him a better fight, no doubt about it."

As the days and weeks progressed after the fight there seemed to be a growing acceptance in some quarters that Sibson had not given of his best. Various boxing pundits claimed that he was disinterested, gave up too soon, didn't try hard enough and others blamed the decision not to spar in the run up to the contest as being amateurish. Even former world welterweight champion John H Stracey joined in the criticism when he penned a letter to the Boxing News claiming that Tony's effort was the poorest he'd seen from a British boxer abroad, suggesting that it had only been about earning money. This drew a response from Tony's loyal friend and former landlord in London, Ray Clewer who argued that Sibson had done his best. It is interesting to review how Hagler performed over the next three years against the world's leading middleweights. He stopped Tommy Hearns and Mustapha Hamsho in the third round. He stopped Wilford Scypion in the fourth. He knocked out Juan Roldan in the tenth and John Mugabi in the eleventh. Only the legendary Roberto Duran managed to last the full distance.

On the night Sibson was well beaten, and he knew it. But, under different circumstances, could he have done better, even to the extent of winning? Providing his nose had healed properly, there should have been more sparring as the fight approached. The long wait in the ring for Hagler, no doubt had an unsettling effect, but it should not have been unexpected. Squires obviously felt though, that given the experience of Tony's manager, Sam Burns, and advisor Mickey Duff, this should have been anticipated better. Tony should not have been allowed to go into the fight with brand new boots on, or wearing a new body protector. Someone should have been in control!

It's all *ifs and buts*, nevertheless, given a different set of circumstances, Sibson may have given Hagler a sterner test. During the fight he occasionally managed to get in close and let go with a burst of hooks. Hagler didn't back off, granted, but that would have been Tony's type of fight. Sibson has never claimed he could have beaten Hagler, but in conversation in later years he has indicated that he'd liked to have taken Hagler into a war. He'd liked to have known, if after a real battle, similar to the bout Hagler would have with Tommy Hearns, who would have taken the decision.

Sometimes the most accurate version of events, whether it's about boxing or everyday life, is directly after an event has occurred. In courts of law great credence is usually given to statements made soon after someone has witnessed a crime. With this in mind, Sibson's interview in his dressing room with Harry Carpenter soon after the fight finished, perhaps gives us the most revealing description of the contest, at least from Tony's perspective. "I'm not kidding anyone in this world, and I'm not kidding myself, I believed in my own heart I could beat him. I know I'm a slow starter, but I couldn't get started! I did start finding my way in after two rounds. He wasn't hurting me but he was so correct, accurate. He wasn't making me buzz, but he was so correct, he was knocking my head back. Listen people are going to criticise me for not sparring, but his arms were very long and very fast. I'm feeling happy, I'm not crying or anything, I was well licked by a master in the ring. I've fought top fighters and broke down their defence, but good tactical boxing ability beat me tonight. I've beaten great champions, but I couldn't find a way to get to Marvin Hagler tonight. I just couldn't find my way in. His reach was very deceiving. I said to him at the weigh-in 'you're not as big as I thought you were,' but I wasn't looking at his arms! Listen the man was very accurate and I just couldn't do anything about it." That just about sums the fight up, doesn't it?

CHAPTER 10

Atlantic City

When life began to settle down after the Hagler fight, Sibson found himself an ex-British champion, ex-European champion and ex-Commonwealth champion. He was also an ex-world title contender with no immediate prospects of a re-match.

Sibson was conscious that brother in law Alan Moore, his partner in the building firm, Michael James Limited, had been carrying most of the burden while Tony was preparing for the Hagler fight, so he was keen to devote more of his time to the business. He was now in a steady relationship with his girlfriend Julie Swift, and a young son, Ryan, made his way into the world. Along with a family dog it now seemed that a *normal* everyday life beckoned, but this relative tranquillity was short lived. Sam Burns and Mickey Duff wanted him back to work in a boxing sense, and a fight was arranged for Wembley on 3 May against top level American Bobby *Boogaloo* Watts. Tony had seen Watts before, when he'd been Hagler's sparring partner at the Craven Arms prior to his fight with Minter. However, in the lead up to the fight Sibson contracted the flu, and the rising West Ham middleweight, Mark Kaylor, stepped into the breach subsequently stopping Watts in the fourth round.

Into this vacuum came a surprise transatlantic call from larger than life American boxing promoter, Don King. Tony couldn't believe his ears. "Hi, Tony Sibson? This is Don King,

I'm going to get you to Deer Lake where the great Muhammad
Ali trained, I'm going to get you a new world title shot." Tony
told him he wasn't boxing anymore and that he was giving it up,
but King was persistent. "You can't give it up, you've still got a
chance." The man known as *Teflon Don*, because nothing
seemed to stick, wouldn't take no for an answer and kept up a
steady stream of persuasion for over half an hour before Tony
was forced to say his goodbyes, and hang up. Albeit uninvited,
this call nevertheless signalled to the downcast Sibson that he
was still a marketable commodity.

Although Tony was retreating from the boxing world, in
early June he was persuaded to attend a meeting of the Leicester
ex-boxers association. Their chairman, Mick Greaves, the man
who had mentioned Sam Burns to Tony, belatedly presented
him with a replica of the Dave Crowley Belt, which had been
awarded by the London ex-boxers association for Tony being
their *Fighter of the Year* in 1981.

For all intents and purposes the publicity shy Sibson had
retired   from   boxing.   He   didn't   make   any   special
announcements, he probably didn't even form this firm opinion
in his own mind, but the way his life was going, his total lack of
interest in the sport meant that if nobody made contact with
him he would probably have drifted so far off the radar that a
comeback might have been impossible.

During the summer Sam Burns had been keeping in touch
with Sibson trying to find out when he'd be willing to get back
into the ring, but he simply wasn't interested. Then Mickey Duff
phoned and he too tried to get the reluctant Sibson to agree to
another fight. Duff can be persuasive and eventually Tony

agreed, with a special proviso, to carry on. Tony told him that he wasn't prepared to take part in routine *ten rounders*, providing the main attraction to *showcase* Duff's new group of young stars coming through. He wanted a big fight, with big money, and made it clear he wouldn't accept anything less.

Frenchman Louis Acaries had won the European title and he was proposed as an option. Sibson insisted that this fight be put out to purse offers, but before this could be concluded, Mickey Duff, who had been weaving his magic, had secured a lucrative pay day in America against rising Irish-American middleweight, John Collins. It is difficult now to reach a conclusion as to what Duff's motives were in arranging this fight. Did the veteran promoter have faith that Sibson could still reach the ultimate goal of winning the world title, and this was the start of the road back? Or, did he simply see an opportunity to cash in on Sibson's name, by putting him up as a beatable opponent for Collins, who was seen by many to be the new face in the middleweight division?

The fight was fixed for Atlantic City on 8 October and Tony went back to the grindstone at the Squires gym in Syston. About three weeks before the fight, with the hard fitness work almost complete, Tony flew out to Atlantic City where he had accommodation in the Playboy hotel/casino complex where the fight was going to take place. With Squires not travelling with him, it might have been suggested that his Leicester trainer was being edged out, but in fact that was not the case. There were good practical reasons for the arrangement. Squires had a full time job and a number of other boxers to look after back in Syston, and he knew this was a great opportunity for Tony to get himself back into world contention. Sibson went out to America with Squires' best wishes.

On arrival in America Sibson soon realised that he'd be trained by his old nemesis from the Mwale fight, George Francis. Also out there at the time were Cornelius Boza-Edwards, John Mugabi and new Leicester professional, Chris Pyatt. But there was a shock in store for the now very experienced Sibson, who remembered very well the situation at the boxing gym owned by Carmen Graziano. "We were training in a place in Vineland at the back of Atlantic City and the gym was rough, I'll tell you! Christ Almighty, they were there to knock your brains out! I'm still fragile and I thought 'What have I come out here for?' My bottle hadn't gone, but there was nobody there that I knew. Everybody was in there, heavyweights were in there, light-heavyweights were in there, all sorts were there. Tasty kids. They were fighters who couldn't sell tickets, but they were getting good pay days for stepping in at the last minute. A couple of times I was sparring I'd touch gloves then, crash, bang, wallop! I was trying to keep it nice, being friends and they were trying to tear lumps out of you! After the first session my heart was about broken, I felt sick and I asked myself 'Is this why I'm back in boxing?' I thought these guys are wanting my scalp. I'm sitting in the Bar one night with Chris Pyatt and I'm eating cheesecake and drinking chocolate – comfort eating really because I didn't know if I wanted to do this anymore. We're talking about what was going on and he was trying to encourage me. I went to my room and rang my dad up. My bottom lip was going and I said to him 'I don't know if I want to carry this crap on.' He said 'Get out there, enjoy yourself, come on!' Well I had a cry, went out there the next day, had my breakfast, had a run and bought a record out a shop. You've got to remember I'd been sparring these kids for a couple of days and I couldn't get it right. They'd been knocking me about a bit, and Mickey's been looking at me and thinking "You're fighting John Collins? What's going on?' Anyway, this day I went in there and smashed them to bits. The gym came alive even more then. They were smashing their hands down on the canvas of the ring and the more they did that the more I whacked them to pieces. I hammered them, the light-heavyweight, the middleweight, then Mickey Duff says 'Right, that's it, George, no more sparring!' I can't remember doing that to anybody before. I went for the heavyweight first and he jumped through the middle rope before the first round was finished. He didn't want to know, I was pumped up. George was looking round the gym for others to spar and telling them to get in and they were all turning their backs, they didn't want to know."

It's quite clear from that account that at some point during his days' training in Vineland the old fire was re-kindled and Tony got his appetite back, and more. That could not have been good news for John Collins! Collins from Chicago was ranked in the top ten by both the World Boxing Council and the World Boxing Association and was being hailed in America as the new star of the middleweight division. He'd won all of his twenty-nine fights, with only three lasting the distance. He towered over Sibson, standing 6'1" tall and the fight was being televised live across America in an attempt to create a greater fan base for Collins and make him a household name. As far as the American promoters were concerned Sibson was simply a stepping stone.

Having watched Sibson in the gym with the sparring partners, Mickey Duff now knew, no matter what his original intentions had been, that the old Sibson was back.

In the Playboy Hotel the night before the fight Sibson was trying to keep his mind focussed, as he recalled "I hadn't sparred for a week and a half and I wanted to taste that action again to reassure myself I was ready." He was sitting alone in the foyer of the hotel when a *lady of the night* approached him looking for business. Sibson could see what was going on and saw the funny side. He explained to her who he was, bought her a coffee, and sent her on her way. The reason he was actually sitting in the foyer was because he was being inundated with phone calls allegedly from the police in Chicago continually asking him if he'd beat Collins. At the same time the hotel was bouncing with Irish-Americans from Chicago singing and dancing with some of them dressed up as Leprechauns! Eventually Tony managed to get the staff at reception to intercept the calls to the room and he did finally manage to get some sleep.

The psychological warfare wasn't over, and at the weigh in the next day, Tony shone some light on Duff's mastery in these situations. "He could look at you and the other guy. This guy's full of beans and he can't wait to give me a good hiding. I'm looking at the floor, I'm pumped up but I don't want to look at him and get myself distracted. But Mickey whispered in my ear 'Take a good look at him,' and I looked up, and you know what, he was finished then. He knew, and I knew, he was going to take a massive beating."

Sibson had George Francis and Mickey Duff in his corner for the first time and, unusually for him, was wearing red and white trunks. He looked extremely fit with not an ounce of fat to be seen. Right from the start he moved in on Collins and didn't give him any time to settle. Tony was trying to draw leads from the American and he did occasionally got through with right hands but they were ineffectual. The impression was that Sibson was just ready to explode into action, and explode he did, with a long right cross which shocked Collins. Sibson sensed immediately that the Chicagoan was in bother and chased him along the ropes throwing left and rights. With only a few seconds remaining in the round Collins seemed to have recovered and pushed Sibson back. But his joy was short lived as a left hook dropped him in his own corner with the bell saving him. His corner men worked feverishly to get him ready for the next round and when the bell went Collins was on his feet and looked prepared, but a right hand put him over within twenty seconds. Once he was back on his feet Sibson launched into the offensive and after several thudding uppercuts the referee called a halt, just as Collins stumbled over and went to ground.

There are strong arguments for suggesting that this was Sibson's best performance. He was fighting a top ten fighter, who was undefeated, and had a very high percentage of knockout wins. He was fighting away from home against an opponent who was being shown on national television right across America in the belief that a new boxing star had emerged. Tony was also the underdog, and had been out of the ring for eight months following a demoralising loss. More important however was how he won the fight. He was very quick, controlled, and didn't waste a punch as long as the fight lasted. He didn't rely on his famed left hook and indeed the fight turned his way with a right cross. It is also worth recording that Collins won five, four inside the distance, and drew one in his next six fights, indicating his quality. The following week Sibson appeared on the front page of the Boxing News under the banner headline *Sibson's Back In The Big Time.*

Tony arrived home two days after the fight and along with his girlfriend made a quick turnaround before flying off for a well earned break in Tenerife. The victory placed Sibson back in the limelight and promoters on both sides of the Atlantic were discussing possible opponents. In America the television people had planned a Collins-Bobby Czyz fight, but following Collins' defeat, the next obvious route was for Sibson to take on Czyz instead. At the same time the European Boxing Union set a deadline date for purse offers for an Acaries-Sibson contest, and to add to the confusing picture the British media were building up a *super fight* with British champion Mark Kaylor.

When the EBU looked at the purse bids they saw that an Italian promoter Rodolfo Sabbatini, jointly with Top Rank from America, had made a record offer for a European title fight of £165,000, 40% of which would be Sibson's cut (£66,000, or £184,000 at 2012 values). Sabbatini wanted to stage the fight in Paris, probably in January. In the meantime the promoters were intent on preparing for a Kaylor-Sibson showdown and arranged for both to appear at Wembley Arena on 22 November. Tony's original opponent was to have been Leroy Hester who in August had stopped leading middleweight contender Wilford Scypion.

Sibson went back to America and trained in Tampa with George Francis under the belief that a fight with Bobby Czyz was being planned. By the time he was advised that a fight had

been arranged in London beforehand, Sibson had contracted a
severe chest infection and couldn't train properly. Francis
suspected that Tony was malingering because he knew he didn't
want the London fight and Tony remembered the trainer telling
him one morning "I know you're not well, Tony, because I
thought you might be putting it on and I followed you to your
door last night and waited outside. I could still hear you
coughing your heart up!"

An added pressure for Sibson was that following his
impressive win over Collins all his Leicester fans were keen to
see him in action, so, reluctantly, a half-fit Sibson travelled back
to Britain. Tony realised he wasn't ready for the fight and
seriously thought about calling it off at the last minute, but he
knew that so many of his supporters had bought tickets and
arranged transport. By now his opponent had been changed to
Manuel Jiminez a Puerto Rican who'd lost his last three fights.In
truth Jiminez shouldn't have been in the same arena as a fit Tony
Sibson, let alone the actual ring. At the weigh in, conscious that
Sibson was grossly overweight, George Francis surreptitiously
caught hold of Sibson's shorts as he stepped on the scales and
gently lifted him up. Tony recalled the needle on the scales
waving one way, then another, and when Francis had judged it
correctly, his weight was announced as 11st 6lb!

The chaos continued in the dressing room before the fight.
Tony saw that his manager Sam Burns was still wearing his
'civilian' clothes and asked him who was going to be in his
corner. Burns replied that he had to sit with his wife because he'd
just bought her a diamond bracelet, and they were having a
night out. He then asked his manager about his purse for the

fight, and Burns told him he'd have to see Mickey Duff about that. Burns did eventually don a red seconds' jacket and assisted in the corner – and Sibson was paid!

In actual fact Sibson started the fight as if nothing was wrong and quickly got the measure of the overweight Puerto Rican, dominating exchanges and looking sharp. However Jiminez was nothing if not durable and took everything Sibson threw at him. There was a repetitiveness about the fight and as it wore on Sibson slowed down, but although still marching forward and landing regularly there was no noticeable changing of pace in an effort to finish the fight early. At long last in the eighth round referee Harry Gibbs had seen enough and brought the one sided contest to an end when Sibson launched a final two fisted attack on the ropes. At ringside, watching his prospective challenger for the European title, was Louis Acaries. There was also a setback for Mark Kaylor, he lost on a ninth round disqualification, his first defeat.

Towards the end of the year the Boxing News carried travel adverts for the Sibson-Acaries fight which now seemed scheduled for 25 February. After his traumatic fight with Hagler in February, and an eight month hiatus, Tony had stormed back with a devastating victory over Collins in October, followed by a routine win over Jiminez, while suffering from illness during his preparations. He had now a very lucrative pay day pencilled in for February and would have been entitled to a period of relaxation and recuperation over the Christmas holiday period. It was not to be!

Tony's backers had been offered another big earner by American television to fight Bobby Czyz in Las Vegas on 14 January. The money put up was £55,000(or £144,000 today).

CHAPTER 11

Lee, Acaries and Kaylor

Bobby Czyz would have been an ideal opponent for Sibson. He was only a couple of inches taller and moved forward constantly, both factors which would have suited Tony. However the projected fight never came to fruition because Czyz, realising that making the middleweight limit had become too much for him, pulled out.

The American television date remained, but as well as a change of opponent, another venue was found. Instead of Las Vegas Tony had to return to Atlantic City. In the opposite corner would be *Dangerous* Don Lee from Wisconsin, and at 6' 2" possibly Sibson's tallest opponent to date. He had been the fourth opponent offered to Duff in three days, and one of them had to be accepted for the event to go ahead. Lee had won nineteen of twenty-one fights and was a completely different proposition to Czyz. Tony was shown a video of one of Lee's fight and thought he was an acceptable opponent. The Boxing News reckoned that this was a good *warm-up* fight for Sibson before his European title challenge to Acaries and thought that Lee was a far easier option than original opponent Czyz.

Sibson told Bob Mee years later how he felt at the time. "When they offered it to me, I said no. I was dead. I couldn't face it. I told Sam Burns, Mickey Duff and Jarvis Astaire, but eventually Mickey persuaded me. I must have been daft. I thought I owed it to them. I thought I should be loyal because we were all a team and they were going to look after me. I really thought that if I pulled out I'd be letting them all down. I can't believe I did it. But Mickey promised me it would be an all-expenses paid trip and that I could take Julie if I wanted to. In the end I took the fight. It was down to me. Obviously Mickey didn't want to lose the big TV date, but nobody put a gun to my head. Of course, it wasn't all expenses paid!"

As promised, Julie and baby Ryan were accommodated with Sibson at the Holiday Inn Hotel in Tampa and he prepared for the fight under George Francis. Once again, contrary to his belief in using sparring as a learning experience, and similar to the events in Atlantic City, he had another gym war, this time with a complete stranger! Again Tony recalled the situation for Bob Mee. "He was black, a good 13st and complete muscle. He wanted to spar with me and I had just finished with Chris Wells and said 'No chance, I've had it.' I didn't know him, but we all thought he was just some hard-case off the street. The next day he came back again and George said 'Just give him a round.' I went out there, looking to take it easy, and he was brilliant. His first punch split my lip and embedded my teeth in it. I couldn't believe it. I thought I'd been set up. The first round he dished it out. I don't like gym wars, I never have, because you don't get paid for that. At the end of the round George called out 'That's enough,' but I didn't even go back to the corner. I was mad, I was spitting blood literally and I shouted out 'One more, one more.' In the second we just laid into each other. It stopped the whole gym. He gave me some good shots again, but towards the end of the second I was getting to him, I felt it. At the end of that one, I yelled out again 'One more,' and just charged in again and did the business. He took it all and still gave me some back, but he'd gone then. We had a street fight. I lost all the pretences and the frills. Then afterwards it just turned out that this man was a world champion kick-boxer who had just come back from a tournament in the East somewhere with $100,000 and a prize car. He was a top class professional!"

Shortly before the fight, the camp moved to the Sands Casino Hotel in Atlantic City, but a real problem had emerged. The old chest infection had returned, and Tony wanted to call the fight off. This was a difficult situation for everybody involved. The venue had sold tickets, the television company had a national time slot and Mickey Duff was guiding Tony towards another world title shot. With all this preying on his mind Tony was persuaded to go ahead with the fight.

At the weigh in Sibson came in at 11st 9lb, usually an indication that his training had been affected. Tony explained his condition in the dressing room before the fight. "How a doctor passed me fit, I've no idea. I was sweating buckets. I was lying practically unconscious on the settee in the dressing room. Less than a minute before the fight I was still on the settee fast asleep because I was ill. When I say a minute, if it was two minutes I'm pushing it. Then I was straight in, I didn't know where I was!"

The contest started well for Sibson because he had Lee down from a short left jab towards the end of the first round. The American came out for the second and he had changed to a southpaw stance. Although Lee came more into the fight catching Sibson with the occasional long left cross he still didn't do enough to win the round. As they came out for the third there was no indication about what would transpire. Midway through the session Lee caught Sibson right on the point of the chin with a vicious left hook and down he went. He got to his feet looking more embarrassed than anything else, but a second left hand dropped him again and this time he was visibly hurt. Just as it looked as if Tony had weathered the storm another flurry of blows forced him to rest on the bottom rope bringing a *standing* eight count from the referee although he protested vigorously that count was unnecessary.

Sibson made a miraculous recovery to take the fourth round and in the corner afterwards he could be heard to jokingly suggest to Mickey Duff that he was giving his promoter grey hair. However, the disaster continued in the next round, when a clash of heads resulted in a gash appearing over his left eye. In the corner George Francis got to work in an effort to bring it under control and Mickey Duff could be heard telling the referee that it was 'superficial'. In the sixth and seventh Lee continually switched stance and both rounds were hard to score. It was ominous however when Duff was heard to tell Sibson in between the sixth and seventh to finish Lee off as he was concerned the American officials might halt the fight due to the eye damage.

The eighth turned out to be Sibson's final appearance in an American ring. Midway through, Sibson appeared to catch Lee with a left and he stumbled to the canvas. The American protested, but was given a count nonetheless. Almost immediately on resumption Dangerous Don threw an explosive left hand punch sending Sibson down heavily. He got to his feet but fell backwards against the ropes and the referee decided he was in no position to carry on. Afterwards Tony tried to tell interviewers that the stoppage was premature but it was clear he was *gone*. The cut eye needed seventeen stitches from a plastic surgeon to close it.

Sibson's experiences over the last eleven months in America had an almost biblical ring to them. Following his *crucifixion* against Hagler he had been *resurrected* by the Collins win but had finally been *nailed to the cross* by Don Lee, which signalled the end of his world title aspirations for the foreseeable future.

In the dressing room after the fight the entire camp was in a bad place, but no one was feeling worse than Tony himself. The plan had always been to fly to Miami afterwards and continue preparations for the Acaries fight, which of course must now have been in extreme doubt due to the cut eye injury. But this was end for the relationship Sibson had with his team in America as can be seen from these comments. "We flew out to Miami and we were due to fight Acaries in about six weeks. Now, I'm looking at myself and my world's falling apart. All the work I've done and two people, who are supposed to love you, have allowed this to happen. I should have been bigger, but I was only a kid. I was at death's door for the Don Lee fight but, no excuses, he was a good fighter. Anyway, we flew to Miami and nobody could talk to me because they don't matter to me anymore, they're finished. Mickey had to go away on some business, John Mugabi was there and I never even got out my bed for about a week. I couldn't train because I was ill, but I was coming out the end of it, the doctor had given me some injections and I got some fever powders then George tells me

I've got to do a bit of training. I went running one day, got back, showered, didn't go to the gym. Put some clothes together, ordered a taxi, took me to the airport and got a flight home. Best day's work I ever done in my life! If I'd stayed out there I'd been smashed to pieces in the Acaries fight, I'd been finished."

Sibson knew that there was only one man could get him ready for the Acaries fight in such a short space of time, so it was straight back to Leicester to seek out Ken Squires. When Tony met Squires he told him how bad a state he was in, but his old mentor calmed him down and assured him he had time enough to get him fit. Sibson took up the reins with relish, enjoying the atmosphere in Syston. He watched the young fighters on the punch bags, seen the old familiar faces and by the middle of February had started sparring with Tony McKenzie and Romel Ambrose. But he admitted that what spurred him on most was the need to prove to Sam Burns, George Francis and Mickey Duff that he could do without them. Outside the ring Tony wasn't treading water, and had bought a new property, a former hunting lodge in Cold Overton near Oakham.

One important matter had to be dealt with first, and that was to have the injured eye checked. So Sam Burns arranged for Squires and Sibson to come down to London. They met Burns at his home and he ordered a taxi to take them to see a plastic surgeon in Harley Street along with Board representative Doctor Adrian Whiteson, and what stuck in Ken Squires memory most about this visit was a relatively minor incident but which meant a great deal to him. "We go down to Sam Burns' house near Lord's cricket ground, a big house, and he orders a taxi. We go down Harley Street, we're getting out the taxi and Burns says "Ken, take care of the taxi!" Do you know what I mean. I've spent £26 to bring him down on the train and this millionaire waves the back of his hand towards me as if I'm nothing and tells me to pay for the taxi." The eye injury passed the inspection and because of concerns the Board had with Sibson's illness in America, they ordered Dr Whiteson to carry out a check on his weight. He was 11st 8 lb, ideal for the week before a fight.

The whole team met up in London prior to travelling to Paris. George Francis tried to be sociable towards Sibson, not having spoken to him since his sudden exit from Miami, but Tony, easily embarrassed with face-to-face confrontations, gave him the cold shoulder treatment. Both Mickey Duff and Sam Burns must have realised from Sibson's manner that he had little time for any of them. Ken Squires remembered that on arrival in Paris they were met like royalty, with their car being guided through the notorious Parisian traffic by motor cycle outriders. The camp was afforded the use of a gym in Paris through old foe Jacques Chinon. It's quite amazing what goes on behind the scenes before these big fights, an aspect to professional boxing which is only known to a chosen few. Chinon had been asked to organise a couple of sparring partners for Sibson, and Ken Squires wanted them to be a bit heavier than Tony. When they arrived at the gym they saw that Chinon had found two French gypsies and they looked a pair of tough nuts. When Squires was slipping on Tony's big sixteen ounce gloves he told him to be careful and to put a couple of heavy shots across their bows early on. Tony did as he was told and before a minute had passed the first sparring partner literally ran out of the ring with Squires chasing him. Ken was determined that his charge would get the sparring he needed but both threw the gloves and head guards down and left the gym without stopping. Squires eventually saw the funny side, but not for a few hours!

Acaries was the same height as Sibson and had won thirty-eight of forty-two fights. Although experienced, there were no world class names on his record, and in his only bout outside France he'd lost in Italy on points for the European light-middleweight crown. He secured the European middleweight title in December 1982 and defended it twice. He was not an outstanding opponent but his backers had put up a record purse bid for this defence so they must have been confident of an upset.

13,000 attended the fight in the new Bercy Stadium in south east Paris with a few hundred travelling over from Britain. The fight was televised live by ITV and because of the needs of the television executives both boxers were kept in the ring for quarter of an hour before the contest got underway. Sibson took the early initiative with a strong sharp jab, which although unable to pierce the tight guard of Acaries, helped him to win clearly the first three rounds simply because the champion hardly threw a punch! From then on, although Acaries landed with the occasional right hand, the fight turned into a tough but predictable brawl, with Tony lacking his usual speed and power in the left hook. Although Sibson was edging the rounds, he was not convincing, and due to the close quarter barging and wrestling his cut eye eventually opened and had to be treated in the corner by George Francis. At the end, the judge's scorecards came in, and Sibson had regained his European title. When the scorecards were examined it was clear that the judges had been watching a different fight to anyone else. The Italian judge gave the fight to Acaries by four rounds to two while scoring SIX rounds even! That meant that he must have scored one of the first three rounds to Acaries or marked it as a draw, when the Frenchman only landed one punch! In fact, out of the thirty-six rounds the judges' scored, they thought eighteen were drawn! Immediately after the fight a relieved Sibson told the press that he had been head-butted by Acaries all through the contest and had been scared the old cut would open and he'd get stopped. In hindsight it was probably the case that the clashing of heads was unintentional. Acaries had a style which meant he moved forward in a partial crouch and as he was the same height as Sibson there was always going to be a possibility that their heads would meet.

In the dressing room after the fight Sibson told waiting British pressmen "I've got lumps and bumps all over my forehead. And my chest bone is sore where he kept ducking and banging his head against me. The worse it got, the worse I got. I didn't feel confident and I was frightened of getting smashed up on the inside because he was a clever so-and-so, a right old campaigner with a lot of experience and a lot of tricks. It wasn't my normal style, but I showed I could box. I was slipping the jab in and was always covering up. He didn't care what he did in those clinches, though, and I was frightened that he would do some damage."

Sibson's performance had been poor in comparison to what he was capable of. The speed, movement, and punching power were simply not there. He was lethargic and as the fight progressed he was, for the first time, looking to clinch and hold on until he could get his wind back. There was no variety to his punches, but even an off-form Sibson had still managed to get one of his titles back.

There was also crowd trouble caused predominately by Sibson fans as the fight ended. Several dozen *skinheads* descended from the upper tiers to the ringside and endeavoured to clamber into the ring itself. Once there, a pitched battle ensued, resulting in a steward firing off a tear gas canister which adversely affected all those still in their seats. The following morning, Bob Mee, who had been covering the fight for the Boxing News gave an example of some of those who attached themselves to the Sibson bandwagon. "On the morning after the Sibson-Acaries fight I woke early, eyes still sore from the tear gas. I got up and went for a walk around the grey, quiet, winter streets on the northern side of the city and towards Montmartre and its white-domed church, the Sacre Coeur. As I turned a corner I heard an awful wailing noise, 'Siiiibbbbbbbboooooo, Siiiiiiiiibbbbbboooo!' I followed it to a graveyard and there, in one of those walk-in shrines with which the French sometimes honour their dead, he sat in tee-shirt and jeans, with a Union flag for a blanket and surrounded by bottles of beer, pouring out the contents of his soul to the morning light."

Once again Tony and family took themselves off to the Canary Islands and on their return he set about working on his new property in Cold Overton. Boxing was taking a back seat and he was quite happy with the rest and enjoyment of not having any pressure with preparing for upcoming fights.

In mid April the Boxing News reported that Sibson would be meeting Juan Domingo Roldan on 7 July at San Remo or Monaco in a final eliminator for Hagler's title, and the audacious Brendan Ingle took out a full page advert in the Boxing News on 4 May, challenging either Mark Kaylor or Sibson to put up their titles against his fighter Herol Graham with a *winner-takes-all* side stake of £10,000. When Ken Squires was reminded of this he recounted the following tale with a huge grin. "We had Brendan Ingle and Bomber Graham up at the gym in Syston for a sparring session with Tony. Now I always thought Graham was a bit of a limbo dancer. Well, he's running round the ring, leaning backwards over the top rope. I saw Tony's attitude change and I knew what was coming. He gave Bomber a few taps and Brendan calls it off, saying 'I thought this was supposed to be a sparring session?'" Squires couldn't remember when this took place but to be fair to Herol and Brendan it's likely to have occurred when Graham was an aspiring light-middleweight and Sibson either approaching, or actually at, world level.

As summer approached Tony would occasionally wander along to the gym in Syston, going for the occasional hill run with the rest of Squires' boxers, and sparring with Tony McKenzie and the others. It was during these sparring sessions that he knew how far off his fitness had gone when he was getting caught by punches he should have been avoiding. Knowing that he was walking around at fourteen stones or thereby necessitated the sweat suit getting looked out but there was no consistent training being done. In addition Sibson had developed a problem with his left elbow. He noticed that if he fully extended it he felt a sharp pain and this was restricting his movement. Without even considering what this meant for his boxing career he knew that he didn't want to spent much longer with this handicap, and had it examined by a surgeon in Leicester. The x-rays showed two fragments of bone within the elbow joint and an operation was recommended.

The big fight for the British boxing public, and one which had been brewing for some time, was a triple title showdown between British and Commonwealth champion Mark Kaylor, against European champion Sibson. By August, the fight date had been settled for 25 September at Wembley and Tony visited Ken Squires to find out if he thought he could get him fit in time. Squires felt that the six weeks would be enough, and gave his assent. But Tony's elbow injury, which they had kept quiet about, flared up, and forced a postponement. Sibson now tried to explain to Sam Burns that the bout should be cancelled until after surgery and recuperation but, once again, his manager and his associates persuaded him that there was a possibility he'd be stripped of his European crown if it didn't take place soon, and Tony reluctantly agreed to go ahead with it.

Mark Kaylor was the 1980s version of boxing's glamour boy of the 60s, Billy Walker. The West Ham middleweight had a huge fan base in the east end of London and there were hopes that he would win a world title. He won the ABA middleweight crown in 1980 and reached the quarter finals of the Moscow Olympics that same year just missing out on the medals. Managed expertly by Terry Lawless he won his first twenty-four bouts, and stopped twenty-one of his opponents. In doing so he stopped former Sibson victim Roy Gumbs to win the British and

Commonwealth belts. In the twelve months since then Lawless had tried to move him up to world level with mixed results. He had lost on a ninth round disqualification to Tony Cerda but then came back and impressively stopped Ralph Moncrief in the fifth. He had another stiff ten round test before meeting the dangerous punching, and aptly named, Buster Drayton. He came unstuck in that one, being knocked out in the seventh. He was an exciting fighter in that he approached his contests like a medieval jouster, with an attitude which said "You knock me down, or I'll knock you down!" If Kaylor got caught cleanly there was a good chance he'd fall, but you can be guaranteed he'd get back up. At the same time he could punch, as around 90% of those in the opposite corner could testify. Just the type of boxer to sell tickets by the barrowload. When the original date was cancelled Kaylor kept in tune with another bout on 16 October when he stopped David Todt in the sixth round.

The boxing press had been clamouring for this fight for over a year and with three titles on the line everyone involved in the promotion knew it was a sure fire money spinner. The fight was re-arranged for 27 November and Wembley Arena was a complete sell out, with dozens waiting outside in the hope that spare tickets would become available. As unusual *Sibbo's Army* had turned up in huge numbers from the Midlands and when the fight got under way it was their *football chorus* which rang round the hall.

As the bout progressed it was clear what the Kaylor tactics were going to be. When Sibson got in close the Londoner's long arms would surround his smaller opponent in an attempt to stifle his work and prevent the left hooks from detonating. He was largely successful but a wicked left hook did land in the second causing Kaylor to stumble and Sibson followed up swinging lefts and rights. At the end of this round Dennie Mancini, who had been drafted in as specialised cut man by Sam Burns, jumped in to attend to a minor graze around Sibson's eye, and although no further damage appeared for the rest of the fight, Mancini maintained this central position! For the remainder of the contest Tony had Squires, Mancini, Burns and Pinchin all in his corner. It was obvious from the BBC recording of the fight that in the later rounds, with Mancini providing most of the inter-round advice, Tony had little interest in what he had to say, looking past him into the distance. This sometimes happens when a boxer's management decide to bring in a virtual stranger at a late stage. When the fight gets tough and tiredness sets in, it's the familiar voice the fighter hears, and with Sibson, that would have been Ken Squires.

The contest was now following a regular pattern. Sibson would bore in, Kaylor would smother, the referee would tear them apart and Sibson would have an occasional burst of punches and Kaylor would hold again. It was not the exciting battle the pundits had expected but it was nevertheless very gruelling for the boxers but there was no doubt Sibson was edging the rounds. The sixth turned out to be Tony's best when another left hook got through and with Kaylor hurt the Leicester man pushed on trying to end it. As the fight entered its last two rounds, Kaylor, who had never been beyond ten, surprisingly began to let loose and a right hand knocked Sibson sideways. Encouraged by this success he launched an all out attack catching Sibson again with a right uppercut.

Both boxers came out for the last intending to have a real go. Sibson looked the most tired and although the round swung to and fro, Kaylor probably took the final session. Because it was also a European title fight, there were two ringside judges as well as referee Coyle scoring the contest. Coyle gave Sibson six rounds, Kaylor four, with two drawn. Judge Larry O'Connell gave Sibson five, Kaylor three and scored four even. The other judge Roland Dakin saw the fight the exact same as O'Connell. Sibson was the unanimous winner, and triple champion for the first time. After the fight Tony told Bob Mee "Mark had bottle. After our fight I felt so sorry for him. I said to him 'You can come again. You've got pride. Don't you pack this game in, you can fight.' I knew I had won the decision, but I said to him 'You're the man, you'll take my place one day.' I don't think he knew the score, he didn't know what my war was. He didn't know it wasn't against Mark Kaylor!"

Nevertheless, life wasn't all serious, at least for Tony's younger brother Sean, still laughing while telling the following story. "Tony had arranged a photo shoot with a photographer from the Leicester Mercury." With beating Kaylor, Sibson had again captured the Lonsdale Belt but he'd not won it outright, so the Boxing Board had to have it back. The day before it was due to be returned Tony wanted a photograph taken with the Belt so he could give it to family members. Sean again took up the story. "He was living out at Cold Overton at the time, and before we went to get the photograph done Tony wanted the house warmed up, so he started trying to light the wood burning stove. He had difficulty getting it going and was throwing cups of petrol on it. Still it wouldn't light. By this time the petrol was obviously lying in the tray underneath. When he put a match to it the thing exploded in a ball of flames and as Tony stumbled back we saw that he'd singed his eyebrows and the front of his hair. Not to be beaten, Tony went and got his hair cropped but if you look carefully at the photo you can see he's got little left of his eyebrows!" *(Sorry Tony, but the photographs in the book!)*

The fight was no sooner over when the Boxing News reported that Sibson's next fight would be a well-paid defence of his European belt early in 1985 against Frenchman Pierre Frank Winterstein. As a result, it appeared that Tony would have to relinquish his British title because the Boxing Board were insisting he fight the number one contender, Herol Graham, by the end of February.

History will show that the Winterstein fight didn't happen, and Sibson would not be inside a boxing ring for thirteen months.

CHAPTER 12

A New Promoter – Frank Warren

When there's sharks in the water, it's a good idea to get out quickly. Easier said than done when you've got an anchor tied round your ankles. In Tony Sibson's case that anchor had the name *Sam Burns* engraved on it. By the start of 1985 Burns had been Sibson's manager for five years and Tony was well and truly sickened with the relationship. He recalled how he had been forced to go through with the Jiminez and Lee fights while suffering from a chest infection, and then he'd to fight Kaylor with a damaged elbow. It was a running sore for Tony with the knowledge that the contract still had twelve months to run.

When Sibson had entered into the initial contract it was on the understanding that Burns was a totally independent representative who would *sell* Sibson's services to whichever promoter offered the most money. Since then, every fight he'd fought in Britain had either Mickey Duff, Mike Barrett or Jarvis Astaire involved in the promotion. How independent from this group was Sam Burns? When Sibson fought Collins and Lee in America Mickey Duff was actually in his corner with George Francis. In fact it was Mickey Duff who offered to bring Sibson's wife Julie and baby son out to Tampa for an extended holiday when he was preparing for the Lee fight. When Tony fought Acaries in Paris, a contest promoted jointly by an Italian and Top Rank based in America, Duff, who had no official role in the fight, can clearly be heard on the television recording incessantly shouting instructions to Sibson during every round.

On 9 December the Sunday Times and the News of the World published details of a contract signed on 11 June 1979 by Mickey Duff, Mike Barrett, Jarvis Astaire and Terry Lawless agreeing that all four should pool their income from their various activities relating to boxing and share the proceeds equally. From Sibson's perspective this showed the close relationship Barrett, Duff and Astaire enjoyed, indeed Jarvis Astaire's company, Jaras Entertainments Ltd, handled the transfer of Tony's purse from the Hagler fight between America and Britain. In 1979 this group were the only ones running major tournaments in Britain, but since then a young Frank Warren had moved onto the scene thereby offering managers an alternative to Duff, Barrett and Astaire.

Herol Graham had been pursuing a fight with Sibson for some time and the constant publicity was annoying Tony. Graham's defensive skills went unappreciated out with his Nottingham and Sheffield base, and he was not a great ticket seller. Sibson didn't feel he had paid his dues to boxing they way others had, and was quoted as saying "The sooner we meet the better. I can't wait to play piano on his ribs. He's the only fighter I know who can limbo backwards under the bottom rope. He knows he can only earn big money by meeting me, but the way I feel about him I wouldn't mind getting him in the gym, locking the doors, and doing the job for nothing."

Into this cauldron stepped Frank Warren. He offered the Sibson camp £60,000 to fight Jimmy Price of Liverpool. Sibson recalled what happened. "Sam didn't want anything to do with me boxing for Warren, even though Graham would stay the number one contender. That fight wouldn't have gone away just because I'd have taken the Price fight. Instead of that they wanted me to take up an offer to fight Buster Drayton, but that was worth only $50,000(£30,000)." When Sibson realised the Warren offer had been rejected he phoned him up. "I said 'Frank, thanks for the offer but they're not playing ball.' He said to me 'Don't you realise he's your employee?' I said 'What are you talking about?'. He said 'You employ him, he don't employ you, you *tell* him you want that fight.'" With the Sibson camp refusing to make the fight Tony had to give up the British title, and Frank Warren won the purse bids to stage a Graham versus Jimmy Price battle for the now vacant crown.

What Warren had said to Sibson about Burns' being his employee, got to the root of how Tony had been feeling for some time. He never fully appreciated how their relationship should have worked. Occasionally Sibson had successfully fought his corner in relation to insisting that fights be put out for purse offers, like the European defences in Bilbao and Paris, plus, of course, the fight with Hagler. But it niggled him when he was forced to take fights in London against mediocre opponents. He felt that those fights resulted from his manager accommodating Duff and the others, to the detriment of himself, when Burns should have been totally committed to looking after his fighters' best interests. Tony now knew that he was losing out on good financial pay days, simply because his manager had taken sides in the rivalry between two factions.

The Drayton fight was set up for 14 April at Wembley to coincide with an America TV date, but Sibson put his foot down. "I told Ken Squires 'I ain't fighting again for that lot. Forget it.' I wasn't bothered if I ever fought again."

Although Sibson had made his mind up, his manager, apparently oblivious to the decision, pressed ahead with arranging another fight. Danish promoter Mogens Palle won the purse bids for a European title defence against Ayub Kalule in Copenhagen on 15 June. For £60,000 Tony would gladly have thought again about fighting under Burns, but this time the long standing elbow injury had to be dealt with. It was giving him constant pain and training was impossible. He later told Bob Mee "I kept leaving it, but in the end I had to have the operation. They completely dismantled my elbow and took out two pieces of bone that were just floating loose in fluid. The surgeon did a good job, but the elbow was knackered. I never threw left hooks again the way I used to and I couldn't throw a jab properly. I learned to adjust the angles of my punches to suit the injury, but it was never the same." As a result of his failure to meet Kalule, Sibson was stripped of his European title.

In November it seemed that the Boxing News had decided Sibson was retired. They published their world ratings and in the middleweight division had Herol Graham at number seven, Mark Kaylor at twelve – with no Tony Sibson! The following week in their European ratings Herol Graham was number one, Mark Kaylor at two, Errol Christie at five, Brian Anderson (Graham's stable mate) was in at twelve, and Jimmy Price was fifteenth, and no Tony Sibson!

As the year end approached the managerial contract was coming to its conclusion. One day Tony got a phone call from Sam Burns. Burns told Sibson that he thought they had six great years together and asked if he wanted to continue the relationship. Tony reminded Burns of how he had rejected the offer of three fights in America before the Hagler challenge, the refusal to put European title defences out to purse offers and how he rebuffed the £60,000 offer to fight Jimmy Price. Tony told Burns that they were finished and the elderly manager slammed the phone down. Tony recalled, "I sat back and laughed. I felt free."

Not only was the contract over, but at that time it looked as if his boxing career was similarly concluded. He was recovering from surgery on his elbow, he got married in June, his weight had shot up, he was unfit, a second son had arrived and he was relishing just being *one of the boys* with his old Leicester pals. He was reasonably wealthy, involved in a building business and was still re-developing his buildings at Cold Overton. There were offers to get the gloves on again, most notably from Mike Barrett who phoned him up and offered a return fight with Mark Kaylor. The money on offer was good, but Sibson just could not be bothered.

Ken Squires entered into this vacuum. Squires worked with Frank Warren through his other boxers and had arranged a meeting with Warren, trainer Ernie Fossey, and Tony. The outcome of this was that Tony would fight exclusively on Frank Warren promotions but would be self-managed. Sibson reached an agreement with Warren for each of his first two fights and compromised when his comeback fight was on the undercard of a light-welterweight title bout involving Terry Marsh.

Bob Mee discussed with Sibson his motivations for returning to boxing in an interview he carried out with him in 1986. He told Bob "I just didn't want to trickle away. I don't want to be an idol or anything, but just being on my own I felt really down. I was sitting around not earning a shilling and I thought 'I've faded out.' I felt lonely, as if everything had been for nothing."

Continuing with the Bob Mee interview Sibson said "I needed a change. But it took something like this to get me out of bed and bopping again. I'm not looking for any favours, but I believe I deserve something after all I've put in. I want the British and European titles again and I want my world rating back, and then another go at the world title. I need one more British title win to get a Lonsdale Belt to keep, and that belt belongs on my mam's mantelpiece. I never used to take care of myself. Boxing was the last thing on my mind. Now I think 'What a fool, what an idiot you've been.' It took this fourteen month break to get me to see it. I suppose I've grown up."

The first fight Sibson had under the promotional banner of Frank Warren was on 22 January 1986 at the Alexandra Pavilion in London. Tony acknowledges that this bout was probably an opportunity for Warren to assess just how much he had left in the tank. In the opposite corner was Juan Elizondo from Mexico. He was not in Sibson's class. He'd been fighting as a professional for fourteen years and had lost twenty-one and drawn three of his forty-nine fights. Under the previous regime Sibson would have been totally switched off with the quality of the opposition and more than likely would have come in to the fight heavy and de-motivated. However, he had the excitement back in his veins and a sizeable following of his fans had bought tickets, no doubt delighted that the show was back on the road. All of which was extremely bad news for the Mexican!

Sibson arrived in the ring resplendent in Leicester blue shorts and dressing gown to the familiar *Sibbo* chants from his loyal fans who seemed to fill the hall. Tony was announced as the Commonwealth champion, the only title he now held. This was a *keyed up* and aggressive Sibson who had weighed in only three-quarters of a pound over the middleweight limit. He looked in excellent condition. Sibson explained his attitude in the lead up to this fight, "I was giving them the two fingers, I felt fantastic!" an obvious reference to his former camp.

Within seconds of the first bell sounding Sibson had Elizondo down, but referee Harry Gibbs thought it was a slip and didn't take up the count. Tony attacked constantly and shook the Mexican several times throwing shortened left hooks to the head and body. In the next round Sibson flattened Elizondo with the trademark left hook. The visitor bravely pulled himself up and if he had any foresight he would have stayed on the canvas. The next assault resulted in a vicious left hook exploding on the Mexican's chin sending him, unconscious, to the deck in Sibson's corner. Ken Squires, seeing the stricken boxer, reached in and took out his gumshield before the referee had signalled the end. A breach of the rules, but a compassionate move nevertheless. An outstanding performance even though the opposition was poor.

With the first fight under the Warren deal now complete, the promoter declared that Sibson's next fight would be a defence of his Commonwealth middleweight bauble against Ayub Kalule on 26 February. But again there was trouble brewing because there was a possibility that Kalule would have to fight Herol Graham in defence of his European title. Warren threatened legal action against *anyone* who put his fight between Sibson and Kalule in jeopardy. None of this was bothering Tony. He was delighted to get back in the groove with a stunning performance and it also looked to everyone that his left elbow had fully recovered.

About a fortnight after the fight Sibson gave an extremely frank interview to Bob Mee. In it he allowed us a brief glimpse into his character when he said "I've got an inferiority complex. I really think I have. I blush. I'm no good in public, always put myself second best in company. I've never gone out much and I turn down functions, not to be rude but because I don't think I'm cut out for that. I can't talk boxing outside the gym. I'd rather donate a pair of gloves or something than go and speak somewhere. I don't like voicing my opinions, generally. Indoors I've got my own rooms where I can be on my own and I'll sit and watch guitarists, the great ones like Hendrix, Clapton and Muddy Waters, for hours. I'm the bloke who used to go down the Polytechnic and watch the guitar players and wish I was them. That's what my kids are going to be. They've got little guitars already."

In the meantime Herol Graham had added the European crown to his British title and it seemed that another Battle of Britain, with three titles at stake, had to happen. For some reason the fight with Kalule fell through and Tony's challenger for the Commonwealth bauble would be Ghanaian Abdul Umaru Sanda. The African was tough, tall but unspectacular. He'd won seventeen of twenty-one fights and the only recognisable name on his record was Sibson's former sparring partner, Cliff Gilpin whom he'd outpointed. Once again the fight was booked for the Alexandra Pavilion in Muswell Hill.

Sibson weighed in at 11st 5lb in the afternoon at Stringfellows night club but Sanda had to remove some excess before he too eventually got under the limit. When they entered the ring it quickly became clear that the Ghanaian would be Sibson's tallest opponent and he looked to be in superb condition. So too was Sibson.

With Ernie Fossey joining Ken Squires in the corner, Sibson started the fight at a fast pace and never let up for the entire twelve rounds. He was fast, aggressive and performed as well as he'd ever done. Tony dominated the entire fight except for one brief scare in the third round when a tremendous left hook from Sanda landed cleanly on his chin. The television slow motion recording of the incident showed that for a split second Sibson was *gone* and although staggered, his tip top conditioning allowed him to recover and by the end of the round he was punching back furiously. Tony was still in full swing in the last round and almost stopped the brave African champion. Taking everything into consideration, and with a challenger who was much better than expected, Sibson was nothing less than outstanding. It was certainly the best he'd been since the Collins fight.

In the ring afterwards interviewer Gary Newbon asked him how he felt about a fight with Herol Graham. Sibson was obviously reluctant to say anything disparaging about a fellow professional but was forced to comment "He's been disrespectful, and said some disrespectful things about me, but I don't want to say anything, I just want to get him in the ring."

Sadly, from the ninth round onwards much of the fight was missed by those at ringside because they were more intent in following the disturbances several rows behind them. Again this was put down to a small minority of Sibson's supporters.

The day after the fight Frank Warren told the media that he'd been trying to get a re-match with Don Lee but the American had just signed for another fight. Therefore, he'd arranged another bout, against top ten opposition in the shape of rising star, Doug de Witt.

Tony never did fight de Witt but Warren kept him moving nevertheless. A new venue in central London at Kingsway, was the Royal Theatre, and it was almost filled to its 1,500 capacity for Tony's next outing on 16 April. In the opposite corner was another substitute, this time in the apparent undemanding form of Puerto Rican, Luis Rivera. He had lost his last two fights inside the distance to top quality middleweight opposition, Lindell Holmes, and coincidentally, Doug de Witt in January.

Once the fight started it became patently obvious that Warren was not intent on bringing in poor quality opposition. Rivera, again towering over Sibson, demonstrated how a tall fighter should deal with a much smaller opponent. He was fit and threw fast punches whenever Tony moved in. Indeed a long right hand opened a cut in the corner of Sibson's left eye in the very first round. In the second a head clash drew an angry response from Tony and the cut worsened. The Leicester man was being caught repeatedly as he moved in and now realised he'd have to put more thought into the fight. Sibson was winning the rounds, just, but he really had to work. In the sixth a solid right hand punch from Rivera caught Sibson square-on in a crouch and he was put down. He looked more embarrassed than hurt when he got to his feet and referee Larry O'Connell didn't even bother to count. The knockdown gave the visitor confidence and he abandoned his counter-punching style and moved onto the offensive. Rivera arguably took the seventh round as well as Sibson tried to figure-out a response, and he did get his act together almost flooring the Puerto Rican in the ninth.

Commentator Reg Gutteridge made an unforgettable analogy when both boxers touched gloves at the start of the tenth round. He said that it reminded him of the pleasantries exchanged by a dentist and the patient prior to starting his drill! So right he was. Sibson came out firing on all four cylinders in an attempt to end proceedings and Rivera had to use all his experience and ring craft to hear the final bell. The result was not in any doubt but Rivera had made a first class effort.

The days following the fight were chaotic for Sibson. On the one hand he was demanding that the fight with Herol Graham be made, and in that regard the eighteenth was the closing date for purse offers for a contest in relation to Graham's defence of his European belt. At the same time Frank Warren announced that he had fixed up a return bout with Don Lee for the 3 August. With this all going off around him, Tony had a more practical matter to deal with – a plastic surgeon had to repair the damage to his cut left eyebrow – and just to keep the pot boiling, he flew off to Jersey as a special guest at an amateur boxing show.

In late May it was announced that Warren, with a bid of £147,000 (£350,000 in 2012) had secured the right to stage the European title fight between Sibson and Graham sometime in September. Strangely, and completely out of the blue, the public became aware of a possible showdown between Dennis Andries and Sibson for the former's recently won WBC light-heavyweight crown.

When Dennis Andries won the WBC version of the world championship there would not have been anyone in British boxing who could have grudged him his day in the sun. He had served his apprenticeship, and more! Born in Georgetown, Guyana, but now from Hackney, Andries had turned professional in 1978, and since that time probably hadn't engaged in a single easy fight. He wasn't particularly tall for a light-heavyweight measuring just over 5' 10" but was extremely strong and durable. He won the Southern area title within a year of turning professional and was challenging unsuccessfully for the British title within two years. He had one other failed attempt at the national crown before winning the right to wear the Lonsdale Belt in 1984. Andries made two successful defences and was then forced to write a personal letter to the Boxing News seeking support for the right to challenge for the European title and more widespread recognition for his efforts. The European chance eventually came in December 1985, but he was held to a draw. He made yet another successful defence of his British title the following February and got an unexpected opportunity to fight for the world championship against an American, JB Williamson, in April.

Andries had a marketability problem! He was awkward and clumsy, lacking in conventional boxing skills and didn't have a large fan base. He'd been successful purely on heart, determination, strength and pride. Characteristics, however, which many boxing fans admired. If you had to pick a man to accompany you into the trenches, you would be unwise not to consider Dennis Andries!

It has to be assumed that the reason why an Andries versus Sibson match was being proposed was that both fighters had connections to Frank Warren. Of course it would allow Sibson to fight again for a recognised world title and also provide Andries with his biggest pay day. So perhaps there was merit in the idea even though Andries' title was the weight above that at which Sibson fought.

The fight was booked for 10 September, back at the Alexandra Pavilion, and it's useful to take a look at how the boxing media saw the fight. The Boxing News examined how Sibson had fared against light-heavyweights in the past including the disastrous loss to Mwale. They firmly believed that Andries would simply be too big and strong, predicting a stoppage win, between the eighth and tenth rounds. Meanwhile, perhaps predictably, Alan Parr of the Leicester Mercury thought Tony's movement and skill would be enough to see him win after a tough contest.

However there were strong indications in the lead up to the fight that suggested Sibson should have been more than capable of at last winning a world crown. His three fights in 1986 showed that he was moving well in the ring, his timing was accurate and he was using his experience to create openings for the big punches. The elbow injury seemed to have healed fully and he didn't appear to have lost any of his punching power. Sanda and Rivera had both landed cleanly with hefty blows but Tony had recovered instantly from these and went on, unperturbed, to win the fights clearly. Andries, for all his physical attributes and extra weight, didn't have the world class skills of many of Sibson's previous victims and surely he would leave openings for the smaller man?

As part of Sibson's preparations, Ernie Fossey had suggested to Ken Squires that there might be a mutual advantage if he sent up a young amateur for a fortnight's sparring. The man sent up was the 1986 ABA middleweight champion, Nigel Benn. Squires arranged accommodation for Benn at a nice hotel in nearby Rothley, and he was uplifted on a daily basis by Tony McKenzie. McKenzie was preparing for what turned out to be a successful challenge at the British light-welterweight title, ten days after Sibson's joust with Andries. The sparring with Benn turned out to be ideal and both men enjoyed the experience, until matters took an unnecessary turn for the worst. A few days before the end of the second week, Benn's trainer Brian Lynch appeared on the scene. Lynch started to change the atmosphere, massaging Benn's shoulders before he went into the ring, treating the forthcoming session as if it was going to be a real fight, and was overheard suggesting that his charge was too good for Sibson. Both Tony McKenzie and Ken Squires described what happened next as a *war*. Sibson suddenly realised that Benn was throwing bombs, and didn't realise what was happening at first. Once the penny dropped, the young amateur knew he'd made a mistake as he got knocked around the ring and ended up with a black eye. When the session was stopped, Benn jumped out the ring and Sibson went over to Squires and said "What was that all about?" Tony McKenzie remembered thinking that Benn's trainer must have been off his head. Benn came back to the gym the following day and all was forgotten.

When they meet up occasionally at boxing functions Nigel always points at Sibson and reminds people that this was the man that *sorted him out!*

Sibson recalled that on the day of the weigh in he felt good and was confident that he'd have enough to beat the champion. Shortly before he was due to step on the scales, and completely without the prior knowledge of both Tony and Ken Squires, his London backers made what turned out to be a monumental error of judgement. Not fully aware of their man's deep sensitivity, they decided to *spook* Andries by using one of the oldest tricks in the book. Just as Sibson was preparing to step on the scales they got him to put weights into his shorts, a move which would have everybody believing that he was much nearer the light-heavyweight limit. Sibson and Squires knew that he was weighing around 11st 12lb, and Tony couldn't believe that people he trusted and respected were behaving in such an *amateurish* way. He shuffled onto the scales and his weight was announced as 12st 4lb. Everybody knew that something was wrong. Reg Gutteridge questioned how he could weigh as much when he looked so fit and trim!

This distraction was all the temperamental Sibson needed for his mind to go into overdrive. As the day progressed he thought more and more about what had happened and became convinced that his team believed he was going to lose. Why else would they feel it necessary to try to gain a psychological advantage?

When reflecting on the Andries fight years later Sibson had these thoughts , "I didn't need the Andries fight. I had distanced myself so much from boxing by now that I didn't know who was there in the middleweight division or any other come to that.

Ken Squires, as ever, was doing his job but when you're mentally not there, it's not going to happen. I had heights in my life which I could never have anticipated especially so young and now it seemed to have become so laborious , the desire had gone. All the hard work was done but it was just finding the zone. I was very destructive to myself. I had always came back after every defeat with a positive result but the dents were always there."

The *full house* signs were up again when the fighters entered the ring with most of the 5,000 in attendance, as expected, shouting for Sibson. The atmosphere was electric inside the packed arena because although Andries was the bookmakers favourite there were many who had witnessed Sibson destroy opponents with his left hook and wondered if those nights would be repeated. A fact not fully appreciated by many, was that the fight was also for the British title. A curious decision, because as this was a WBC world championship contest, it would be scored by the referee and two ringside judges, while in those days British fights were still marked by the referee on his own!

There was no *feeling each other out* in the first, as both boxers fought aggressively in an effort to dominate the other. Each of the first three rounds was close and could have been scored either way. Former world champion John Conteh, interviewed while sitting at ringside, thought Sibson was looking good and was ahead as far as he was concerned. In the fourth, two clumping left hooks seemed to unsettle Sibson and probably edged the round for the champion. The next round was even until the very last few seconds when a left uppercut from Andries staggered Sibson.

Previous page: 11: Gym members at Syston showing off their new equipment courtesy of Bernard Hart of Lonsdale Sports – Mickey Bell, Mickey Kidd, Tony, Ken Squires, Troy Sibson and Kevin Squires. *12:* Sibson practising his timing on the speedball in preparation for Hagler. *This page: 13:* Promotional photo of Tony and Marvin Hagler.

14: Tony preparing for Acaries fight in Paris. *15:* Sibson using his defensive skill to avoid a left hand from Frank Tate – 7 February 1988. *Photograph by kind permission of Action Images.*

16: The photo Tony didn't want included – notice the singed eyebrows!!!!

Surprisingly, Andries took his foot off the gas in the sixth allowing Tony to dominate and while a few left hooks landed they didn't have much effect. Again Conteh was interviewed and this time he felt that the fight was swinging towards Andries. He felt that Sibson's punches were simply bouncing off the champion, adding that he didn't think Sibson would last the distance. At the start of the eighth, although most thought that Andries was ahead, the job was far from over and the large Sibson support was still optimistic that Tony could win it. That all changed half way through the round, when suddenly, the wild swipes from Andries were thudding home without reply. During a clinch in the middle of the ring Sibson let out a roar and it was assumed by the ringside commentators that he was angry at Andries' use of his elbows on the inside. In fact, on hindsight, it was more likely that it was the first sign of frustration from Tony because he just couldn't ignite the spark that was needed to put the pressure on Andries.

The ninth was a disaster for Sibson, much worse than the sixth against Hagler and the eighth with Don Lee. In that round with Hagler Sibson was able to fire back in bursts after being put down for the first time, and in the Lee fight Tony was put down and eventually stopped after taking full blooded knockout punches on the chin. Against Andries he was clubbed to the deck by punches he would normally have blocked or avoided. At one point he sank to the canvas simply because Andries was leaning on him. On another occasion he sagged to the floor from a half hearted swing by the champion and when he got to his feet he roared at himself again trying to generate some inspiration. Just as Ken Squires was shouting at the referee to stop it, another long right hand, which this time landed with some force on the side of Sibson's head, knocked him to the ground and the referee then decided he'd seen enough. Dennis Andries had done his job in a workmanlike fashion and deserved the acclaim. Sibson has remembered, a poignant and private moment the following morning at a press conference, which summed up the endearing character of Andries. "Dennis, in an effort to comfort me, said 'Tony, do you want to try the belt on?' He meant it from his heart. I said 'You're the champ, that's yours!'"

Afterwards Tony admitted that he had perhaps under-estimated Andries and offered no excuses. He said that he'd often sparred with men around the 13st mark and had little difficulty with their extra bulk, but Andries was different. Some people tried to get him to admit that it had been a mistake to take the fight at light-heavyweight in an effort to encourage him to keep going, and to return to his normal weight division. But it was clear from his attitude that in his own mind his boxing career was over, and more significantly, part of him was pleased that the defeat gave him the opportunity to finally bring the curtain down.

The day after the fight Alan Parr at the Mercury interviewed Ken Squires who had this to say "After the defeat by Marvin Hagler, I thought there were some things we did wrong, but not this time. Tony was in great shape but he just didn't get any of the moves going. I don't know whether it was just the extra size or in fact whether the occasion gets to him. Perhaps fighting for the world title is too much. I'm not knocking him but perhaps he's destined to be the nearly man when it comes to the biggest prize?"

Sibson has a private motto for himself. "If you can't do it, don't say it!" He makes no excuses for any of his defeats, he always maintains that on each occasion the best man won. Nevertheless he had a personality which must have had a drastic impact on how he performed.

With an understanding of this, it is easier to accept why during the Hagler fight he suddenly lost his focus and began to wonder what a lad from Belgrave in Leicester was doing in front of all these famous people. It is also now within the realms of possibility, that the perceived lack of confidence shown by his handlers when they slipped weights into his shorts before the Andries weigh in, affected him so much that it acted like cold water being poured over a fire.

Sibson recalled how he felt at this time. "You know, when you're a fighter, you can look magnificent, like Charles Atlas, but if your mind is not in the right place, if you're not in the room, then you've got nothing. A pudding would beat you. Every time something happens to you, like getting beat, you're dented. And the dents mount up and I knew the dents were there. I didn't want to fight ordinary boxers, no disrespect to anyone, but I didn't want to be someone who just filled the bill. So after the Andries fight I was finished with boxing. It was gone."

In the autumn of 1986 the Tony Sibson boxing story seemed to have reached the end, and if he'd announced his retirement there and then, nobody would have been surprised, nor would they have complained. But the final chapter had yet to be written.

CHAPTER 13

Lonsdale Belt

As sure as the sun rises in the east every morning and sets in the west to close the day, every boxing career moves along the same inevitable path. Tony Sibson's *sun* was certainly dropping behind the horizon, and it seemed to those who knew him, and to those who had followed his career, that it would soon set for ever. The new dawn in the middleweight division had brought Herol Graham, Mark Kaylor, Errol Christie and Brian Anderson.

When the 1987 calendars were opened, Graham was the European champion, his friend and stable mate Brian Anderson had just won the British crown, and Sibson, who hadn't formally announced his retirement, still held the lightly regarded Commonwealth trophy. Those responsible for the Commonwealth competition had nominated Errol Christie as challenger to Sibson, but he'd suffered a heavy knock out defeat in December in a fight watched from ringside by Sibson. With this defeat the possibility of a match with Christie had gone out the window.

There was one hugely motivating factor stopping Tony from finally calling it a day. It was made of a red, white and blue cloth fixed inside a gilded belt with an enamelled photograph of a twentieth century member of the British aristocracy, Lord Lonsdale. This boxing belt, awarded to British champions, and which became their possession once they've won three title fights in the same weight division, has a certain aura in sporting circles. The intrinsic value of the belt depends on when it was made, because that affects its gold content, and who was the original winner of it, but to most its monetary worth is of little consequence. It's simply a cherished possession for those fortunate enough to have one of their own.

One day, Ken Squires and Tony met up, due to the speculation about whether he'd retired or not, and the possibility of him fighting Anderson. Squires said to him "Now listen Tony, I've got to have a word with you about this British title fight. If you win the British title three times you get that Lonsdale Belt outright. The amount of service you've given to the British Boxing Board you should have a Lonsdale Belt. You can get one on the next fight. I know Brian Anderson. I've been up Sheffield to their gym, I know him and you'll knock him out. Bad arm or no bad arm, you'll knock him out. You want to come in to training and I'll get you as fit as I can get you for a British title fight, you'll win the Lonsdale Belt and you'll be able to give that to your father and mother, or whatever you want to do with it. If you leave boxing without a Lonsdale Belt you'll be a mug!"

Tony was persuaded, and decided to give it one last throw of the dice. Frank Warren soon got into action and bid £30,000 to win the right to promote the fight. Although Tony's Commonwealth title would also be on the line, his share of the purse would come to only £12,000 (£27,500 in 2012). Originally the fight was scheduled for 22 April at the Royal Albert Hall, but shortly beforehand Tony pulled out with a viral infection. Warren re-arranged the contest for 27 May but this date too was scuppered and Sibson explained the reason. "I'm getting fit, and all the rest of it, and I felt a little twinge in my calf and I exaggerated it because I knew in my head I wasn't there. I looked great, strong, but he was a capable fighter and my head wasn't right. I just couldn't do it, it was terrible. I got back to the gym from my run and Ken gave it a massage. I went to Brian Wright, a physio down in Leicester, but that made no difference, and the fight was called off."

Worse was to follow for the troubled Sibson. With the stress removed by the fight being postponed, he drove into Leicester the night the postponement was announced to meet friends and try to relax. He had a few pints and on his way home was stopped by the police, refused to take a breath test, resulting in an automatic disqualification. Naturally the rumours started that Tony was leading the high life, burning the candle at both ends and that the fight was called off because he wasn't training. The truth was that the old mental demons had reappeared, his confidence had been jolted, the pressure mounted and he knew he wasn't in the right frame of mind to fight anyone, let alone the highly capable Brian Anderson.

The fight was re-arranged a third time for 17 June, and again it was cancelled. On this occasion it was Anderson who pulled out, injured with a week to go. It was becoming a standing joke amongst the boxing fraternity and nobody now could believe the fight would go ahead until the boxers were actually in the ring.

However promoter Warren would not give up and the fight was re-arranged yet again, this time for 16 September, still at the Royal Albert Hall. Sibson trained hard for this fight although Ken Squires now admits that Tony's left arm was showing signs of wear and tear. When Tony expressed any concern about this, Squires kept his confidence up by suggesting he could beat Anderson with one arm! As the fight date approached the temptation to pull out once again was very real. A few years later he told Bob Mee "I was terrified. I couldn't bear the thought of losing. I couldn't cope. I was down to the weight, but I was being torn up inside. I'd always promised myself that I wouldn't go out losing, but I really didn't know if I could do it anymore. Anderson didn't really worry me, but I was scared to death of the whole thing. I didn't sleep for two days and nights before the fight. I just couldn't get off. The night before I cracked and rang room service and ordered a great big pot of hot chocolate. I was supposed to be drying out. If Ken had known he'd have done his nut!"

It can only be speculation as to what kept Sibson's eye on the ball while in this state. One reason must have been his burning ambition to win a Lonsdale Belt outright, with the knowledge that this might be his last chance to do it, and also the company at the gym, and support of his loyal trainer.

Anderson, the British champion, was a product of the burgeoning Wincobank gym in Sheffield run by Brendan Ingle. Ingle had unconventional beliefs about how boxers should be trained, many of which were frowned on by others. He emphasized the logically sensible idea of not taking punches unnecessarily. This resulted in the unusual spectacle, for that era, of his fighters moving round the ring with their arms down by their side, swaying backwards over the top rope to avoid punches and throwing punches from bizarre angles. His star fighter up till then was of course Herol Graham, who Ingle gave the ironic nickname, Bomber! Graham had annexed the British and European middleweight titles and was undefeated before he moved training camps from Sheffield to Belfast. Brian Anderson was a close personal friend of Graham and had similar mannerisms in the ring to the other Wincobank boxers, but he was much more of an orthodox fighter. While he could move round the ring well and sway out of trouble he tended to keep his hands up and punch *normally*.

Anderson stood 6' 1" and started out in his career weighing just over the welterweight limit. He seemed willing to fight anybody, anywhere in Britain and Europe, and had mixed results. Over the years he settled into the light-middleweight division and fought mostly at area title level. His performances began to improve, and in 1984 he made an unsuccessful challenge for the British title, losing on points to Sibson's Leicester travelling companion and occasional sparring partner, Chris Pyatt. Since then Anderson had grown into the middleweight category and it's possible that Brendan Ingle had kept him at the lower weight due to the growing success of Graham at the division above? Anderson went over to Belfast in October the previous year and beat Tony Burke to win the British belt. Overall he had been in thirty-eight fights, winning twenty-seven, losing eight and drawing the remainder.

When Tony arrived in London for the fight his mind had been in turmoil for months, and in the preceding days it had simply got worse! Ken Squires and Tony travelled down on the morning of the fight, with the weigh in scheduled for 1pm at Stringfellows night club. They were half an hour late due to heavy traffic on the motorway. Again the general boxing public and his legion of fans had no idea about how uncomfortable Sibson was feeling, this great fear of losing, in what may well have been his last fight in front of all his fans, friends and family. To this day Sibson has no idea what happened to put him back in the *zone*, as modern sports stars often say. But back where he should have been, in terms of attitude, was where he most certainly was when he climbed through the Royal Albert Hall ropes to face Anderson.

The champion came out in the first round clearly with the belief that he was taking on a *shot* fighter. He took the fight to Sibson and this suited Tony to a tee. In the second round Sibson's army erupted. Anderson was caught by a couple of hooks and a final left knocked him to the floor in obvious distress. He bravely climbed up on shaky legs. Anderson clung on for dear life as Sibson tried to finish it and he just managed to get to his corner at the bell. Sixty seconds weren't enough to recover from that, and Sibson chased him from pillar to post trying to end it. A right hand landed near the bell and Anderson almost went over again as the referee moved closer as if he might step in to stop it.

By the fourth round Anderson seemed to have recovered his senses and the fight settled down, with Sibson still doing the attacking, and Anderson trying to land heavy shots of his own in a forlorn attempt to stem the tide. In the fifth and sixth Tony looked as if he'd taken his foot of the gas in an effort to conserve energy, allowing Anderson back into the fight to the extent that he started to speak to Sibson and motion with his gloves inviting Tony into a battle. Apt advice to Anderson at this time might have been *when you find yourself in a hole, stop digging!*

Sibson would later admit that in these two rounds he lost his concentration and the old self doubts emerged. Sadly for Anderson, between the sixth and seventh rounds Ken Squires had strong words for Sibson. He told him "Listen, get out there and put paid to this Brian Anderson. You can win this with your bad arm, never mind the arm, get out there and let go. Double left hook or single left hook, roll into him and let him have a left hook. This is about winning a Lonsdale Belt now get out there and do it!" Ken Squires had hit the *on* button! Sibson came out launching quick, strong jabs most of which were landing cleanly. These created an opening and a left hook exploded onto Anderson's jaw and he collapsed sideways to the canvas. If it hadn't been a title fight the referee might well have stopped it then and there. But Anderson pulled himself up on unsteady legs as Sibson piled in. Almost a dozen unanswered bombs landed, and as the referee belatedly moved in Anderson slumped down again. The fight was over, Sibson was back with a bang, and the Lonsdale Belt was assigned to the Sibson family for eternity.

Even in the ring, just after the fight ended, Sibson's fragile state of mind came out when he told interviewers "I felt beautiful for three rounds, but I ran into a mental, nervous problem. I went quiet for two rounds but seemed to be gathering confidence at the end. My corner kept me alive tonight. At the end Brian was holding on for dear life but I can't blame him. He is a courageous man." There should always be some sympathy when a champion losses his title, and this devastating defeat for Anderson may have had a profound effect on him, because he never fought again.

When the belt was placed round his waist Tony added "It's mine now and I'm a better man for it. I suffered more in this fight with nerves than in any other, even the comeback fight after Hagler. I can say it now because he can't benefit by it, but I've waited getting on for ten years for this. I was the youngest man to win a Lonsdale Belt at 21 and now it's mine for keeps at 29!"

Sibson can still recall his feelings about that fight. "When I watch that fight I can't believe my eyes. I never thought I was in front. I had a bad shoulder injury. I done it before the Dennis Andries fight. I didn't tell anybody but I couldn't jab properly. Then when I watched the fight I'm landing with these long jabs, and I couldn't remember a thing. I went through that fight blindfolded. I never seen a thing! I done the ducking and diving naturally and I remember throwing a wild left hook once and that's all I could remember. I got the Lonsdale Belt and I felt so relieved. Bless Frank Warren, any promises he made me, he kept them. I've got to say that. In all my career that fight and the Frank Lucas fights were my best, I get so emotional when I think about them"

Hindsight is wonderful, because armed with this valuable tool the user can never be wrong. It's easy now to suggest that following the Anderson victory Tony should have taken a few days to himself and then announced his retirement. He had fulfilled a lifelong boxing dream in securing a Lonsdale Belt. He had given a ring performance up there with his best. He had business interests outside boxing and a settled family life. He was relatively wealthy and in good health, indeed given the number of fights he'd engaged in and the punches he had taken he was unmarked save for imperceptible hairline scars on his eyebrows. More importantly, when looking back, people would remember him from his last fight – a resounding championship success!

There were other factors to consider, however. His promoter Frank Warren had seen Tony perform better than anyone could have expected and knew there were big fights he could arrange. The Sibson fan club expected him to fight on and believed passionately that their man could go on to win a world title. This was supported by the fact that Hagler had retired and there were now three versions of the title open for challenges. With the rave reports about the Anderson fight ringing in his ears, is it any wonder that he might have been persuaded to carry on?

Immediately after the fight Warren told Paul Jones at the Leicester Mercury "I now hope to get Tony a shot at the world title. We are not really interested in the European title" adding that he'd be holding a press conference on the matter the next day. Tony himself joined the general consensus, still dripping with sweat in the dressing room. "I feel capable of lifting the crown to add to my Lonsdale Belt."

The world middleweight title was in total disarray. With Hagler losing to Sugar Ray Leonard, and Leonard announcing his retirement immediately thereafter, the World Boxing Council, the World Boxing Association and the International Boxing Federation wasted no time in arranging contests for their versions of the title. In fact all three contests for the vacant crowns took place in October. Frank Tate beat Michael Olajide for the IBF title, Sumbu Kalambay beat Iran Barkley for the WBA belt and Tommy Hearns destroyed Juan Roldan in four rounds for the WBC segment. Warren could see the opportunities, and to be fair, on the back of the Anderson performance, Sibson had a realistic chance against all three, with Hearns being the one to avoid if possible.

In late November Tony and Ken Squires met Warren in a restaurant on the M1 and a deal was struck for a world title challenge. A few days later Warren announced that Tony would meet the IBF champion Frank Tate in February possibly at a venue near Birmingham. Sibson and Squires watched a tape of Tate beating Troy Darrell the previous July and Tony had these thoughts at the time about the match up. "I wasn't overawed by what I saw. Long armed, tall kids have never scared me. If I can get up for it mentally, like I did against Anderson, I'll beat him. I'm sure I will." Once again there is the interesting phrase for a world title challenger – *if I can get up for it mentally*. It would seem that the inner confidence from the Anderson win was not well established and the fragility was still in the background.

Sibson and Squires got back into their old familiar training regime at Syston with Tony McKenzie and the occasional visitor supplying variety when it came to sparring. Looking back now, Ken Squires thought that Tony was not as committed to the training as he had been in the past. There were some mornings when excuses were made not to go on his usual run and his eating would sometimes get out of control, but nevertheless he was getting fit, and on schedule for the fight.

There were unfortunate, and important, distractions over the months leading up to the contest. The IBF still had their championship bouts over fifteen rounds duration, while the British Board, under whose jurisdiction the fight was being held, had reduced this to twelve. For weeks on end neither party would budge and the British Board was on apparently solid ground as their rule was based on medical safety. As the challenger, Tony was in the most difficult position because if the bout was not sanctioned by the Board, Tate and the IBF could simply walk away with his title intact. It cannot be encouraging to commit yourself to a strict and exhausting training routine when there is a doubt that the fight might not take place.

In addition, as the pressure of the fight was building inside him, coupled with his discomfort when dealing with the media, Tony made some hasty comments to the Daily Star about his relationships with Sam Burns, Mickey Duff and Jarvis Astaire. Shortly afterwards The Daily Star and Tony were served with writs for libel by Duff and Astaire. Not the sort of issues a fighter needs as he's preparing for a huge fight!

In the meantime Tony had seen a recording of Tate beating Olajide for the IBF title and altered his opinion of the champion. "It's done me good seeing that. He's a far better fighter than he looked against Darrell. Now I know I've got to work." Sibson also tried to harness the bitterness he felt about the libel action and channel that into an aggressive spur to his training.

The fight had been fixed for the Midlands on 7 February but at the highly unusual setting of the Bingley Hall in Stafford. But as the fight date fast approached the crisis surrounding the amount of rounds didn't abate. The British Board threatened to discipline any licence holder who took part and banned their officials from participating. Warren suggested promoting the undercard himself under British rules and then having a different promoter working with IBF officials for the championship bout. NBC-TV from America and the ITV were covering the fight and the Boxing News called it "The biggest political row to hit British boxing in decades!"

Tony was being telephoned virtually non-stop by people wanting to know if the fight was going ahead, and six days before the fight said "Politics is killing this fight for me. At last I've got a title fight and some people are trying to put the boot in. I wish people would leave me alone for five minutes. All I want to do is think about Frank Tate and how I can beat him."

Tate had a fine pedigree. He'd won the gold medal in the light-middleweight division at the 1984 Olympic games, turning professional soon after. In twenty-one fights since, he'd won them all, twelve inside the distance. Tate had fought once before in Britain on the undercard of Terry Marsh's world title win in a tent at Basildon. The fight in March 1987 resulted in a stoppage win over perennial loser Winston Burnett, who to be fair, seldom lost before hearing the final bell. Then, of course, came his title winning effort against Liverpool born, Canada raised, New York domiciled Michael Olajide! Long right hands from Tate had Olajide down and almost knocked out on several occasions. Frank Tate was at the very top of his game and a world class operator.

Everything about Tate was thoroughly professional. He had an excellent team around him when he quietly arrived in this country to be accommodated in the luxurious seclusion of Eccleshall Castle just off the M6. He trained daily at an amateur gym in Stafford with the heating on full blast. Midlands referee Jim Pridding told Bob Mee "It was like a hothouse. Tate worked out with Jesse Reid or his brother Thomas. And never once did he come forward. He worked all the time on the retreat. They trained to drain the strength out of Sibson, to wait, to draw him in, to counter. The whole fight was planned, rehearsed and re-enacted again and again."

Eventually, virtually the day before the fight, and after a court hearing, the British Board won the right to have the fight reduced to a twelve round contest and gave permission for their officials to be used. The delay caused by this debate resulted in the Bingley Hall not being filled to capacity. Fans didn't want to commit to buying tickets if the fight might not go ahead.

The weigh in, again unusually for a title fight in the 1980s, was held the night before. Tate shocked everyone by coming in two pounds overweight. He was given time to get it off and when he got back on the scales Ken Squires made sure he was able to see the dial. The troubled Sibson almost received the spark he needed when he was leaving. As he was walking past Tate he could hear him remark to an interviewer that Sibson had been a good ambassador for boxing but "he's finished now." Sibson remembered his anger at this. "I wanted to reach over. I wanted to slap him, but I reserved myself because of the TV. I wanted to bash him to pieces. If I had done something meaningful like that it might have tipped the scales in my mind. It would have exposed all that work Ken and I had done in the gym, but it didn't."

Tony was interviewed by ITV just before the fight and alluded to having been stabbed in the back by so many people and that this had acted as an incentive for him to be at his best. While he was being interviewed he had no idea that the country roads between Leicester and Stafford were severely congested with fans making their way to the fight, some of whom were spoiling for trouble. One journalist witnessed a van load of fans jumping out with iron bars and destroying the car in front. The first those inside Bingley Hall knew what was brewing was when there was a surge of fans into the main arena just before the big fight, clearly intent on causing disruption. Soon after, someone let off a CS gas canister, leaving ringside guests and sports commentators, including Henry Cooper and Nigel Benn weeping uncontrollably from the effects. The elder statesman of British boxing himself had to take to the ring and call for behaviour. The Sports Minister, Colin Moynihan, who was at ringside added "It's tragic that this should have happened. It's on live TV to the United States. It's very depressing and will require a full investigation by the Board of Control."

Sibson, with Squires and Jimmy Tibbs in his corner, came out looking determined, and showed no signs of the turmoil having had any effect. During the first two rounds Tate looked tentative and Sibson seemed to be boxing a controlled, sensible fight. Tony could well have taken both these sessions. By the third Tate was starting to find the range with his jab and scored with wide left hooks when in close. The fourth was a big round for Tate when with a burst of right crosses and hooks he had Sibson wobbling. The importance of this was that both Tate and Tony now knew the champion had the power to hurt him, while at the same time Sibson had yet to put doubts in the Texan's head. The fifth was much the same as the third with Tate's jabs winning him the round. In between rounds Ken Squires could be heard shouting to Sibson to "Stop feeling sorry for yourself." Either those words had an effect on Sibson or Tate decided to change his game plan, because, boxing behind a quick jab, with the occasional burst when Tate was cornered, Tony appeared to win the next two rounds and by the start of the eighth the fight was probably even. Certainly ITV commentators Reg Gutteridge and Jim Watt thought that the fight was very·close, speculating that perhaps Tate wasn't doing enough to retain his crown. The eighth was a big round for Tate, when he came back into it with long jabs and the occasional right cross scoring cleanly. The fight was lost for Tony mid way through the ninth. Probably those at the venue and watching live on TV didn't appreciate the sudden change. After a not particularly powerful burst of punches from Tate, Tony could be seen stepping back and dropping his arms as if to shake off the fatigue. From that moment on he hardly threw a punch and started to back off every time Tate moved forward. At one point, and unusually for Sibson, he complained to the referee when Tate punched him on the back of the head. One of the morons, who no doubt had disrupted the proceedings earlier, thought it would be a great laugh to throw a banana skin into the ring, and there can be no doubt that he wasn't intending Frank Tate to slip on it!

Very few people would have realised that when the bell rang to signal the start of the tenth, that they'd be witnessing Tony's last round in a boxing ring. It started much as the ninth had finished with Sibson moving backwards with Tate attacking. It's clear now that Sibson's heart was no longer in it, but the final punch, a right hand thrown from way back, landed flush on Tony's chin and would have flattened any middleweight in the world. Sibson fell onto his back, and like the scenes in later years when Mike Tyson was left in a similar position after being felled by Buster Douglas, he was so disorientated that he was left fumbling about trying to put the gum shield back in his mouth. There was no need for a count, the fight, and Tony's career, was over.

After the usual announcements were made Ken Squires told Tony to take the microphone and tell his fans he was retiring. When interviewed in front of the cameras Sibson appeared as if a huge weight had been lifted off his shoulders. He was relaxed, calm and spoke honestly about the fight. He disowned the troublemakers and stated clearly that he personally knew almost all the fans who followed him regularly and they would not have been behind the disruption.

In the dressing room later he said "I just melted away after the eighth round, it was a weird feeling." He added "It was like running for a bus and knowing you're going to miss it. You see it pulling further and further away. I had to work for everything I did tonight. Nothing came naturally at all. I never once felt it was flowing. In the sixth round my supporters helped me dig a little deeper. I was feeling tense and mixed up all night, but they kept me in there and I'm just sorry for everybody that it didn't work out right in the end. I was in great shape physically, but tactically it disappeared. It wasn't the fight I'd trained for. He kept me out and I started to reach for the body, and once I started to reach he could get me with right hands over the top. I gave him too much room, and that gave me too much time to think about the fight and it slipped away. Jimmy Tibbs was really working hard in that corner with Ken Squires and kept saying to me "You're the world champion" and I kept trying to tell myself too. But I never felt right. I slipped the right hand a couple of times at the end, and I thought 'One of those is going to kiss me in a minute' and it did."

It is likely that what Sibson was trying to explain was the loss of his reflexes, an attribute needed at the top level in any sport. For most of his career Tony had moved, parried blows, counter punched and put together combinations without thinking. These skills had been honed in the gym and when fight night came his body responded to situations in the ring automatically. But nobody can hold back time and as the body gets older reaction time slows down almost imperceptibly. If you are a tennis player and this happens you just lose games. If you're a sprinter you lose a fraction of a second off the blocks and your time drops. As a boxer you start to take punches previously avoided and the mind sees openings the body can't respond to quickly enough.

Like every top boxer, once the initial recovery period had past, Tony noticed that something was missing in his life, and although he had wanted out of the boxing game for years he couldn't resist thinking he could give it one last blast. He didn't want to go out on a defeat and looking around believed that a final attempt to regain the European title against the holder Christophe Tiozzo was a realistic possibility. He started running again and as the weight came off made an unsuccessful attempt to contact Tiozzo's management. The phone calls were never returned and the desire faded.

A truly exciting twelve year career came to an end leaving Sibson healthy, wealthy and a whole lot wiser. It had taken him from Digbeth Civic Hall to Massachusetts, Atlantic City, Tampa, Bilbao and Paris. He'd become a household name, a recognisable celebrity well beyond his Leicestershire roots and gave tens of thousands of boxing fans more than a few great nights. Well done!

CHAPTER 14

Conclusion

Most people, when they get to a certain age, can't wait to retire. Even though they might like their work, there are days when the imagination takes over and they visualise holidays in the sun, golfing every day or just simply relaxing and doing just what they want for a change. But retirement is not always what it's cracked up to be. You can't go on holiday all the time, it's not always sunny, the golf course might be unplayable and doing nothing can become boring. People who have worked all their lives usually need to do *something*, that's why it's better to retire with a plan.

Tony retired from boxing just short of his thirtieth birthday, and although he probably didn't see it this way, he had prepared the way for life after boxing with just such a plan. He already had the building business with his brother in law, Alan, his family was settled in Queniborough, and then Thrussington, and he still had the same friends from his teenage days. His three children Ryan, Nathan and Jody were virtually in private education given that the local primary school only had sixty odd pupils, so the immediate future looked pretty settled.

It was very obvious during Tony's career that fame and fortune hadn't changed him. He was the same brother, son, dad, and pal that he'd always been and, except for a brief spell in London, had never ventured much beyond the Leicester city boundary. He cherished all this, because that was who he was, and he didn't want to be anything different. Such is the nature of the man that he doesn't like to discuss his personal finances, but he can't deny that boxing left him wealthy, and as sister Karen and brother Sean suggest, he didn't throw his money away!

Quite rightly, once his boxing career was over, he felt that his life should be private, and this would ensure that all those mental demons which tortured him during his career could finally be put to rest. To a greater extent that is what happened, but of course every now and again invites would appear in relation to some boxing function, and these were generally well received. Even as late as 2012, twenty-four years after his last punch, he was still being asked to appear on television along with Herol Graham and Alan Minter on a Gary Newbon chat show. On several occasions Tony's been invited to functions to meet his old nemesis, Marvin Hagler, and he's become friendly with Roberto Duran through similar events.

In retirement Tony developed a love for sea fishing, sailing off the coast at Weymouth with good friends, a pastime he often enjoyed with dad, Keith, in his advancing years. He also indulged himself in what perhaps is his first love, music. He often travels with personal friends in the band, Kasabian, when they're on tour, and his children jokingly refer to him as the *oldest groupie in the world*. This just typifies the contrast in the man. He's perfectly happy holidaying in Lanzarote with friends including lifelong buddy, Mickey Bell, and the following week he could be travelling the world with a massively famous pop group!

Sadly, of course, grandfather Wally, dad Keith, and old mentor, Jim Knight have passed on but all of them managed to witness Tony win the British title, indeed tough old Wally attended the Lucas fight in his wheelchair. Every fight Tony had in Britain was treated as an outing for his fans many of whom were regulars of the Gipsy Lane Hotel in Leicester, which was virtually the unofficial headquarters for the Sibson fan club. Buses were organised, tickets bought (Tony and his family can vouch for the fact that they never, ever, got a free ticket for any of his fights!), time was taken off work, tee shirts were printed, banners painted and there would be a right good sing-song on the way. It's easy to imagine the excitement.

This partly explains how difficult it was for Tony to walk away from boxing when he was struggling to cope with the attention he was getting. His sister Karen reckoned that if it wasn't for the influence of their dad, Keith, who had such a strong personality within the family, Tony's career would not have lasted as long, or have been as successful.

Tony believes that the greatest night of his career was the victory over Frank Lucas. He, as we've seen, was brought in at late notice, and the underdog. Sibson was just a young lad at the time with no real thoughts about winning titles and had a *carefree* attitude to boxing, which sadly for him was soon to evaporate. After that it all became much too serious, more impersonal, more of a business.

In the same vein his worst night was the knockout defeat by Mwale. Although Tony remains disappointed by his performances against Andries and Tate, particularly the Andries defeat, the loss to Mwale was devastating for everyone connected to him. Such was the momentum building due to his successes up until then, nobody even considered the prospect of the young

Sibson losing, never mind being knocked unconscious in the very first round. His brother Sean, when pushed to give his thoughts on the events that night, remembered that the immediate family, including dad, Keith, were more concerned by Tony actually losing the fight than any medical effects the knockout blow might have had. Sean believes that they didn't even consider any physical damage because they were so shocked that he'd actually been beaten.

After sixty-three professional fights, and over a hundred amateur bouts, Tony is virtually unscathed. His memory is as sharp as a tack, his nose is straight, his eyebrows are the same as everybody else, and, as alluded to previously, he only has a few thin scars on his eyelids. His hands, the tools of a boxers' trade, are undamaged. The only real problem he experienced was with the floating pieces of bone he had removed from his left elbow. Not bad for such an aggressive type of fighter.

In the foreword to the book, Bob Mee speculated that if Tony had been fighting today, with the proliferation of world boxing organisations, he would certainly have won one or other of their versions of the championship. It is also worth considering the fact that since those days, the new super-middleweight (12st) division has become an exciting and often glamorous addition to boxing heritage. Out with title fights, Sibson usually fought around the 11st 9lb mark, and when he took on Dennis Andries at light-heavyweight, he genuinely was hitting the scales at just under twelve stones. Not having to meet the middleweight limit would definitely have been to Sibson's advantage.

Sibson was a physically strong boxer, that was his biggest asset. In the early part of his career, when he was either in an abattoir or a building site he could quite easily have been a *power-lifter* such was his strength. He became a full-time fighter when he moved to London, and while Freddie Hill tried to teach him the finer aspects of professional boxing, Tony himself knew this type of training was doing nothing for him. That's why towards the end of his sojourn there, he began to get odd jobs through friends on building projects. On his return to Leicester it was no surprise that Ken Squires became his trainer and Squires knew what Tony needed, and what had been missing. That's why Ken Squires always spoke about preparing Sibson for the *real* boxing training which was to follow. In other words, Ken had to build up his strength, his greatest attribute. Reg Gutteridge and other media pundits thought chopping wood prior to the Hagler fight was a publicity stunt, a gimmick. It wasn't, it was an essential pre-condition for Sibson before the technical aspects could be worked on.

Tony came fully under the watchful eye of Squires prior to his fight with Bobby Coolidge in September 1980. He won his next nine fights, before running into Marvin Hagler. In September 1983, after training for weeks with Squires, Sibson moved out to Atlantic City and demolished Collins. He came home to beat Jiminez and then went back out to America, without Squires, and lost to Lee. Once again, under the control of his old trainer, he won his next five fights before losing to Andries. By the time the Andries and Tate fights came around it can be argued that the strength gained from hard manual labour had gone, replaced by the routine grind of traditional gym work and running, which was not ideal for Sibson.

Of course this might seem like excuses for defeats, and

remember Sibson himself doesn't put them forward, but there are several people whose views can be relied upon who felt that Tony was well capable of beating both Andries and Tate. The fact remains that he lost to Mwale, Smith, Finnegan, Hagler, Lee, Andries and Tate with his only re-match being against Eddie Smith, in a career which lasted two months short of twelve years. Nobody makes excuses for boxers when they win, and Tony had victories when he wasn't just quite right, but behind every one of those defeats, except the Mwale loss, there was something wrong in the build up.

We all have our favourite Sibson performances, perhaps Lucas or Minter might be up there, but the two round destruction of John Collins, the skills demonstrated against Abdul Umaru Sanda, and the incredible re-birth against Brian Anderson will long linger in the memory.

Sibson's boxing life was an incredible journey from the backstreets of Leicester to rarely seen popularity even among sporting icons of his day but his greatest achievement, and one which he didn't even need to try hard at, was that he came out the other end as the same simple, honest, Bardolph Street lad who started out on his eighteenth birthday.

Tony Sibson Fight Record

Date	Venue	Opponent	Result
09.04.76	Charlie Richardson	W TKO 2	Digbeth Civic Hall
06.05.76	John Breen	W PTS	ArdenS C, Birmingham
26.05.76	Liam White	W PTS	Wolverhampton Civic Hall
14.07.76	Jimmy Pickard	W PTS	Wolverhampton Civic Hall
10.09.76	Bonny McKenzie	W TKO 7	Digbeth Civic Hall
22.10.76	Clive Davidson	W PTS	Digbeth Civic Hall
03.11.76	Neville Esteban	W PTS	Caister-on-Sea
30.11.76	John Breen	W TKO 5	Dudley Civic Hall
14.12.76	Tim McHugh	W TKO 4	Gala Baths, West Brom
11.01.77	Tony Burnett	W PTS	Wolverhampton Civic Hall
19.01.77	Roy Gumbs	W PTS	Solihull Civic Hall
10.02.77	Arthur Winfield	W TKO 2	Tiffany's, Coventry
25.02.77	Tashy Jones	W KO 1	Digbeth Civic Hall
24.03.77	Bonny McKenzie	W KO 7	De Montford Hall,Leicester
07.04.77	Steve Walker	W PTS	Dudley Town Hall
21.04.77	Tony Burnett	W PTS	Liverpool Stadium
27.04.77	Sonny Kamunga	W PTS	De Montford Hall,Leicester
18.10.77	Pat Thomas	D PTS	Wolverhampton Civic Hall
08.11.77	Wayne Bennett	W PTS	Gala Bath, West Brom
30.11.77	Oscar Angus	W TKO 6	Wolverhampton Civic Hall
23.01.78	John Smith	W KO 5	Wolverhampton Civic Hall
06.03.78	Errol McKenzie	W KO 2	Wolverhampton Civic Hall

31.03.78	Mac Nicholson	W KO 7	Liverpool Stadium
23.05.78	Lotte Mwale	L KO 1	De Montford Hall, Leicester
29.06.78	Danny McLoughlin	W KO 3	Wolverhampton Civic Hall
18.07.78	Bonny McKenzie	W PTS	Wakefield Theatre Club
12.09.78	Keith Bussey	W TKO 8	Wembley Conf. Centre
24.10.78	Eddie Smith	L PTS	Royal Albert Hall, London
07.11.78	Gerard Nosley	W TKO 7	Wembley Empire Pool
05.03.79	Eddie Smith	W PTS	Wolverhampton Civic Hall
10.04.79	Frank Lucas	W TKO 5	Royal Albert Hall, London

(Vacant British Middleweight Title)

15.05.79	Al Clay	W TKO 7	Wembley Conf. Centre
26.06.79	Jacques Chinon	W TKO 8	De Montford Hall, Leicester
09.10.79	Willie Classen	W KO 2	Royal Albert Hall, London
06.11.79	Kevin Finnegan	L PTS	Royal Albert Hall, London

(Defence of the British Middleweight Title)

29.11.79	Robert Powell	W TKO 1	Liverpool Stadium
22.1.80	James Waire	W PTS	Royal Albert Hall, London
04.03.80	Chisanda Mutti	W PTS	Wembley Empire Pool

(Vacant Commonwealth Middleweight Title)

03.06.80	Marciano Bernardi	W PTS	Royal Albert Hall, London
27.09.80	Bobby Coolidge	W KO 7	Wembley Arena
08.12.80	Matteo Salvemini	W KO 7	Royal Albert Hall, London

(European Middleweight Title)

27.01.81	Norberto Cabrera	W PTS	Royal Albert Hall, London
17.03.81	Andre Mongelema	W PTS	Wembley Arena
14.05.81	Andoni Amana	W PTS	Bull Ring, Bilbao

(Defence of European Middleweight Title)

15.09.81 Alan Minter   W TKO 3   Wembley Arena
          (Defence of European Middleweight Title)
24.11.81 Nicola Cirelli   W KO 10   Wembley Arena
          (Defence of European Middleweight Title)
21.02.82 Dwight Davison   W PTS   NEC, Birmingham
04.05.82 Jacques Chinon   W TKO 10   Wembley Arena
          (Defence of European Middleweight Title)
14.09.82 Antonio Garrido   W RTD 8   Wembley Empire Pool
11.02.83 Marvin Hagler   L TKO 6   Worcester, MASS, USA
          (Challenge for WBC and WBA Middleweight Titles)
08.10.83 John Collins   W TKO 2   Atlantic City, USA
22.11.83 Manuel Jiminez   W TKO 8   Wembley Arena
15.01.84 Don Lee   L TKO 8   Atlantic City, USA
25.02.84 Louis Acaries   W PTS   Bercy Stadium, Paris
          (Challenge for European Middleweight Title)
27.11.84 Mark Kaylor   W PTS   Wembley Arena
*(Defence of European Middleweight Title and challenge for British
                    and Commonwealth Titles)*
22.01.86 Juan Elizondo   W KO 2   Alexandra Pavilion, London
19.03.86 Abdul Umaru Sanda W PTS   Alexandra Pavilion, London
          (Defence of Commonwealth Middleweight Title)
16.04.86 Luis Rivera   W PTS   Royalty Theatre, London
10.09.86 Dennis Andries   L TKO 9   Alexandra Pavilion
   (Challenge for WBC Light-Heavy weight Title and British Title)
16.09.87 Brian Anderson   W TKO 7   Royal Albert Hall, London
      *(Challenge for British Middleweight Title and defence of
                       Commonwealth Title)*
07.02.88 Frank Tate   L TKO 10   Bingley Hall, Stafford
          (Challenge for IBF Middleweight Title)